IMAGES OF WAR

# TANK WRECKS OF THE WESTERN FRONT 1940-1945

US Army M4 Sherman burning on the streets of Leipzig in 1945.

# IMAGES OF WAR

# TANK WRECKS OF THE WESTERN FRONT 1940-1945

## RARE PHOTOGRAPHS FROM WARTIME ARCHIVES

### ANTHONY TUCKER-JONES

Pen & Sword
MILITARY
AN IMPRINT OF PEN & SWORD BOOKS LTD.
YORKSHIRE – PHILADELPHIA

First published in Great Britain in 2019 by
Pen & Sword Military
an imprint of
Pen & Sword Books Ltd
Yorkshire – Philadelphia

ISBN 978 1 52674 154 7

Typeset in 12/14.5 Gill Sans by
Aura Technology and Software Services, India

Printed and bound in XXXXX by XXXXX

Pen & Sword Books Ltd incorporates the imprints of Pen & Sword Aviation, Pen & Sword Family History, Pen & Sword Maritime, Pen & Sword Military, Pen & Sword Discovery, Wharncliffe Local History, Wharncliffe True Crime, Wharncliffe Transport, Pen and Sword Select, Pen and Sword Military Classics, Leo Cooper, The Praetorian Press, Remember When, Seaforth Publishing and Frontline Publishing.

For a complete list of Pen & Sword titles please contact

PEN & SWORD BOOKS LIMITED
47 Church Street, Barnsley, South Yorkshire, S70 2AS, England
E-mail: enquiries@pen-and-sword.co.uk
Website: www.pen-and-sword.co.uk

Or
PEN AND SWORD BOOKS
1950 Lawrence Rd, Havertown, PA 19083, USA
E-mail: Uspen-and-sword@casematepublishers.com
Website: www.penandswordbooks.com

# Contents

# Introduction: Blitzkrieg And Beyond

Armoured warfare on the Western Front during 1940–5 fell into three very distinct phases: the fall of France in 1940, the Normandy campaign in 1944 and the Ardennes offensive of 1944–5. In southern Europe neither the Champagne, Riviera nor the Italian campaigns were particularly characterized by tank battles.

In the opening stages of the Second World War in Western Europe the German victors regularly posed with and photographed destroyed Allied armour. After the invasion of France the Germans left 4,500 smashed French tanks in their wake, which proved to be a source of endless amusement for happy snappers. Once the tide turned in 1944–5 following the momentous D-Day landings it was the turn of wrecked and burnt-out panzers to be photographed by the victorious Allies during the key battles for Normandy and the Ardennes.

Despite popular perceptions, at the outbreak of the Second World War France had some of the finest tanks in Europe. French armour was certainly equal in quality and quantity to that of the Germans. France's military collapsed in May 1940 not because of poor tank resources but the inability to use them effectively against the Wehrmacht. Defeated France found herself divided in two, the northern half occupied by Germany and the isolated southern half run by a puppet French government from the resort town of Vichy. France was authorized to maintain only an 'Armistice Army', with no heavy equipment, and its Navy.

During the First World War France had almost been the first country ever to produce a tank and was only just beaten by Britain. Its early assault artillery, little more than guns in steel boxes, was at best crude but led to the highly successful Renault FT-17 light tank. A new production programme during the rearmament of the 1930s ensured France had far more sophisticated light, medium and heavy tanks than Britain or Germany and with the best armament.

France even pioneered the first armoured division with the Division Légère Mécanique (DLM – light mechanized division) combining tanks, armoured cars, motorized infantry and artillery. In 1939 it formed the Division Cuirassée (DCR), its first real tank division and by the following year had three DLMs and four DCRs.

The Char B1 tank, supported by some of the older Char D2, constituted the main striking force of the DCRs, while the H-35/39s, R-35/40s and S-35s equipped the DLMs and the light battalions of the DCRs.

While the French had some excellent tanks, the myriad of different types, compared to Germany with just three, proved a logistical problem. For example French ordnance officers were faced with tanks ranging from the tiny Renault FT-17 through the modern Somua S-35 to the heavy Char B1s. Also the design of French tanks resulted in crews feeling isolated from each other. The French mind-set was to treat tanks as armoured cavalry, using them for reconnaissance and screening work. Added to this was a lack of training and importantly tank radios.

The failure to co-ordinate effectively with the rest of the French Army was to have one simple outcome. When war came France's armoured divisions were too dispersed in defensive formations, air cover was non-existent (thousands of French aircraft remained on the ground at safe airfields) and French anti-tank guns remained in storage. France's armoured forces became the first tank casualties of the Western Front.

The events in France in May 1940 were a serious blow to Britain's armoured forces. The British Expeditionary Force (BEF) fared little better than the French Army. In the wake of Dunkirk Hitler captured almost every tank the British Army possessed and most of its motor transport. The Wehrmacht's haul of abandoned equipment included 600 tanks and some 75,000 motor vehicles, as well as 1,200 field and heavy guns, 1,350 anti-aircraft and anti-tank guns, 6,400 anti-tank rifles, 11,000 machine guns and tens of thousands of rifles.

The defeat of the BEF also caused the British Army a serious technological setback. The priority became making good losses, which resulted in all technological development of new weapons being suspended while industry churned out those designs already available. By 1941 the Germans had begun to create a noticeable qualitative gap that the British were never able to close throughout the Desert War.

The British Army went to war with wholly inadequate anti-tank guns, principally the 2-pounder (40mm) developed in the mid-1930s and the 6-pounder (57mm) developed in the late 1930s, though the latter did not enter production until 1941 because the War Office insisted on replacing the 2-pounders lost in France. These weapons were quickly outgunned by the German 50mm and 75mm guns. By early 1942 prototypes of a 3in (76mm) weapon firing a 17lb shot were in hand and by May 1942 the 17-pounder gun was introduced. Hurriedly fitted to 25-pounder field gun carriages, as the spilt trail carriage was not ready, about 100 were rushed to the Mediterranean to counter the appearance of the German Tiger tank in Tunisia the following year.

By mid-1944 the 17-pounder had become the mainstay of the anti-tank regiments of the British and Canadian armies. It had been hoped as early as 1942 to use the Bishop, the self-propelled 25-pounder gun based on the Valentine chassis, as a mounting for the new 17-pounder, but this was not possible and instead the British Army ended up with the Archer variant, with the gun facing to the rear. While far from perfect, 665 of the latter were constructed in 1944–5.

Between 1940 and 1945 Britain churned out 24,800 tanks, a figure comparable to Germany, but nowhere near the massive numbers achieved by America and Russia. Britain's initial star was the Matilda II of which 3,000 were built before production ended in 1943. The tank's armour proved its greatest asset in North Africa against the Italians, but it was ultimately let down by its poor armament.

The British Commonwealth also did its bit for the tank effort. Between 1939 and 1945 Canada produced 1,420 Valentines, most of which went to Russia, and 2,000 Ram and 250 Grizzly tanks (American M3 and M4 respectively). Most of the former were converted to armoured personnel carriers for use in Europe. The Canadians also built 2,150 Sexton self-propelled 25-pounder guns which used the Ram chassis.

The number of tanks produced by Britain's factories would never have been sufficient to meet the requirements of the British and Commonwealth armies. There can be no hiding from the fact that British-designed tanks were not up to the job and the British Army would not have overcome the Wehrmacht but for the supply of American tanks. These were the M3 light, M3 medium and the M4 medium tanks. In particular the latter was supplied in such numbers that it outnumbered all other British-built types combined.

The new British-designed Comet tank was delivered in December 1944 and some saw action the following January. Unable to take the 17-pounder, it was armed with the almost equally capable Vickers 77mm. Due to the slow development of the 17-pounder-armed Challenger, Britain developed the Sherman equipped with the same gun known as the Firefly, which was introduced in June 1944. In the event only small numbers of Challengers were used in North-West Europe, as the Sherman Firefly proved more successful. Likewise some American M10s in British service were also armed with the 17-pounder and were dubbed the Achilles.

During the war America's factories spewed out 88,410 tanks, as well as 18,620 other armoured fighting vehicles based on tank chassis. All this was achieved from a standing start. American tank building went from just 330 in 1940 to 29,500 at its peak in 1943. The Detroit Tank Arsenal, which was constructed from scratch, between 1940 and 1945 accounted for 25 per cent of all America's tanks – producing over 25,000 vehicles.

The best-known of course was the universally famous M4 medium Sherman, which succeeded the M3 series Lee/Grant in early 1942, and first saw action with the British Army in North Africa. In total the M4 made up about 50 per cent of all American tank construction. Although the lighter tanks, such as the M3 and M5 series, were built in considerable numbers in the opening stages of the war, eventually the Americans, like the British and Soviets, largely dropped light tanks in favour of medium armour.

During 1940–1 it was German leadership as much as equipment that gave Hitler his dramatic victories across the length and breadth of Europe. Daring and audacity were the hallmarks of the Wehrmacht's Blitzkrieg, which so successfully unhinged the defences of country after country. Hitler' generals defeated opponents who were more numerous and generally had the qualitative edge in armour. By 1942 the over-engineered excellence of the panzers reigned supreme. The Allies had one simple solution to this: swamp them with a few designs that were easy to mass-produce. Germany could not win a war of attrition.

In the run-up to the Second World War, despite German rearmament, the Wehrmacht had just 5,420 armoured fighting vehicles, of which only 530 were Panzer IIIs and IVs. To resist the German invasion of France, British and French forces were able to pit 4,000 tanks against 2,800 German ones. They still lost. When Germany then turned on Soviet Union the Red Army had 17,000 armoured vehicles in its inventory: they were also crushed within weeks. In light of these figures the Blitzkrieg tactics of the German Army look even more awesome. Ultimately though it was industrial muscle that was to sway the day in favour of the Allies.

Hitler failed to grasp the urgency of the looming tank race. In 1940, prior to the Germans' titanic struggle on the Eastern Front, they produced just over 1,500 tanks. By 1944 they were turning out almost 8,000 a year, but by then it was too few too late. Total German tank production amounted to about 25,000 plus another 12,000 assault guns and self-propelled artillery. The upshot was that the panzers could not sustain their momentum on the Western Front and the initiative passed to the Allies.

In Normandy in 1944 the Germans mustered a total of ten panzer divisions and one panzergrenadier division totalling 160,000 men equipped with just over 1,800 panzers. In addition to this there were another dozen or so independent panzer units, mainly of battalion strength, with a further 460 panzers. This gave an accumulated strength for Army Group B's 7th Army, Panzer Group West and the various Panzer Corps commands of around 2,260 tanks.

By the time of Operation Goodwood on 18 July 1944 Allied tank strength stood at almost 5,900 and continued to rise, reaching almost 6,760 a week later when Operation Cobra was launched. When the Germans commenced their ill-advised Avranches/Mortain counter-attack against the Americans in early August, the American Army could muster almost 4,000 tanks. Allied industrial muscle meant that losses were quickly replaced. For example three British armoured divisions were able to shrug off their losses following two days of intense fighting during Operation Goodwood; replacements arrived within 36 hours.

This book is designed to provide a fascinating visual guide to the fate of the numerous types of tank employed by the American, British, French and German armies on the Western Front from 1940 to 1945. It acts as a companion volume for *Tank Wrecks of the Eastern Front 1941-1945* also published by Pen & Sword Military.

# Photograph Sources

The images in this book are sourced primarily via the author's extensive collection, the US National Archives and Photosnormandie.

CHAPTER ONE

# Hotchkiss

In the late 1930s French tank forces were hampered by competing military interests, a problem that affected all European armies. France's tank units came from differing arms of service, the army's initial tank force equipped with infantry tanks, the chars de combat, and the formerly mounted cavalry regiments. They inevitably had differing views on how tanks should be deployed. Doctrinally the French struggled with how best to use their tanks: on the eve of the German invasion they were only just putting together four dedicated armoured divisions.

In 1940 French tanks were on the whole superior to their German counterparts. The powerful Char B1 bis and Somua S-35 were certainly better armed and armoured. The drawback was that French tanks, especially the infantry support ones, were notoriously slow. Also France's light tanks lacked radios, the main armament had to be operated by the commander and they lacked range thanks to small fuel tanks.

To compound matters for the French army, and the reason Hitler's panzers were able to run circles round it, was that except for the French armoured divisions equipped with the Char B (two battalions each of sixty-eight tanks) and the fast Hotchkiss H-39 light tank (with similar numbers) most of the chars de combat battalions were scattered throughout the army in a support role.

The French Hotchkiss-built H-35/39 light tank constituted one of France's most numerous tank types in 1940. It first entered service in the mid-1930s and by the time of the Second World War over 1,000 had been built for the French cavalry divisions, so was widely photographed following the fall of France.

## H-35

Thanks to the enormous success of the two-man Renault FT-17, the French military were enamoured of the light tank concept. The two-man Char Léger Hotchkiss H-35 was a contemporary of the Renault-built R-35. While the latter was procured to equip French infantry units the H-35 was mainly issued to the cavalry – hence the light tank requirement. Confusingly both tanks were very similar in appearance and carried the same armament, comprising a short-barrelled low-velocity 37mm SA 18 gun and a coaxial 7.5mm machine gun. Some 100 rounds of 37mm and 2,400 rounds of 7.5mm ammunition could be carried.

The H-35's cast turret made by APX was identical to that installed on the R-35 and R-40. Although it was equipped with a traversing cupola, the commander had to climb in through a small hatch in the rear of the turret. This hatch could be folded down horizontally to be used as a seat when the tank was not in combat. The driver accessed the vehicle via a double hatch in the front of the superstructure and the glacis.

The cavalry understandably wanted a tank that was fast and this came at the expense of the armour. On the H-35 it was 34mm thick whereas the R-35 had 45mm of protection. The Hotchkiss tank employed a similar suspension to the Renault. This though had six road wheels either side compared to the five on the R-35, which provided better cross-country performance at speed. Notably the H-35 only had two track-return rollers either side whereas the Renault used three. Also it utilized coil springs rather than rubber washers. Some 400 H-35s were produced with three-quarters issued to the cavalry and the rest going to the infantry.

## H-38

Inevitably upgrades led to newer models of the Hotchkiss tank. Most notably the rear-mounted 75hp engine was replaced with a 120hp one at 2,800rpm, which boosted the speed from 17.5mph to 22.5mph. Although this interim model, known as the H-38, had a more powerful engine, it still retained the ineffectual short 37mm gun. As a result it looked very much like its predecessor, but for one important difference, more of which below.

## H-39

The third version, the H-39, was upgunned with a long-barrelled 37mm SA 38. To accommodate the new engine in both the H-38 and H-39 required elevating the rear engine deck. This is the best way to tell the H-35 from subsequent models. The H-35 engine deck sloped downwards toward the rear of the tank, whereas on the H-38/39 it was raised and almost level, giving the hull a new shape. Nonetheless the various models looked essentially the same from most angles and only the longer gun barrel gave a clear indication that it was a newer model.

Armour was a maximum of 40mm. An external fuel tank could be attached along with a detachable skid tail. The latter was intended to improve cross-country performance. Production of the H-35/H-39 series totalled about 1,000 tanks, of which 821 were in front-line service. This meant that there were plenty to by photographed be the victorious Wehrmacht in 1940.

German troops posing on a Hotchkiss H-35 light tank. This model is identifiable by the sloping engine deck at the rear. The suspension and six road wheels are partially obscured by the grass, but the front drive sprocket and rear idler are clearly visible.

More German soldiers with another captured H-35. Some 400 of this particular type were built. Again note the sloping engine deck

Rear view of a H-35 showing the suspension arrangement. The Hotchkiss light tank only had two upper track-return rollers, whereas the Renault R-35 had three.

This appears to be the interim H-38 tank. This was fitted with a larger engine hence the raised engine deck, but it retained the short 37mm SA 18 gun

An H-38 abandoned at the roadside. Although the Hotchkiss tanks were reasonably fast, they were thinly armoured. The tank has been hit and penetrated through the rear armour.

A field full of captured H-38s. The cast turret made by APX featured a traversing cupola, though this was not a hatch and access for the commander was via a hatch at the back of the turret.

*Above:* This H-39 is recognizable from the raised rear engine deck and the longer-barrelled SA 38 37mm gun. The scissor-type suspension was common to many French tank designs during this period.

*Opposite above:* The Hotchkiss H-35 series featured a double hatch arrangement for the driver which hinged in opposite directions mounted in the superstructure and glacis. This H-39 also has the engine deck lifted to give access to the engine.

*Opposite below:* This H-38/39 had shed its right-hand track and ended up in the ditch. The main turret gun has been removed.

*Above:* An H-38, with the raised engine deck and short-barrelled gun – the French simply did not know how to get the best out of their superior tank force in the face of Hitler's highly co-ordinated Blitzkrieg.

*Opposite above:* German troops being briefed on the capabilities of the H-39. Numbers of captured Hotchkiss tanks were redeployed by the German Army for local internal security operations.

*Opposite below:* Another abandoned H-39 – although the turret is facing backwards the longer 37mm barrel is just visible.

# CHAPTER TWO

# Renault 35/40

The Renault-built R-35/40 light tank was the French Army's most numerous tank type in 1940. Almost 2,000 were built with about half in front-line use. Renault's other tanks included the AMR 33/35, AMC 35, the rarer D-2 and the First World War vintage FT-17.

## R-35

The Char Léger R-35 was designed and built by Renault to succeed its enormously successful FT-17 light tank. The latter had seen action during the First World War and had been widely exported. By the late 1930s large numbers were still in service in France and around the world. The French army had called for a replacement in 1934 and the manufacturers Delaunay-Belleville, CGL, FCM and Renault were all asked to bid. Renault was quick to produce a prototype designated the ZM based on its previous Auto-Mitrailleuse de Reconnaissance 1935 Type ZT light tank.

The ZM had 30mm of armour but this was boosted to 40–45mm on the production vehicles. This meant that the specified 8-ton weight rose to 10 tons. Hitler's reoccupation of the demilitarized Rhineland in 1935 made French rearmament an urgent priority. The ZM went into production with an initial batch of 300 and once in service was re-designated the R-35. By 1940 1,600–1,900 had been built. Whilst production was not sufficient to completely phase out the FT-17 in the infantry tank regiments, it still equipped some twenty-three tank battalions.

As its designation implies, the tank appeared in 1935 as a two-man light tank weighing just under 10 tons. The one-man APX turret was armed with the same 37mm gun and machine gun as the Hotchkiss H-35. The spent cartridge cases from the machine gun were caught by a chute and then dumped through a hole in the floor. This was an attempt to avoid showering the driver in hot brass.

The R-35's role was to re-equip the tank regiments assigned to the French infantry divisions and it was therefore heavily armoured. Its armour was thicker than that of many other countries' medium tanks. This increased weight meant that the Renault four-cylinder 82hp engine struggled to give the tank a speed of just 12mph on the road. While this was fine for keeping up with the infantry, it robbed the tank of any real tactical mobility. The driver was served by twin opposing hatches similar to those on the H-35, that were hinged on the glacis and the superstructure.

Although the layout of the R-35 was largely conventional, castings for the turret first pioneered on the FT-17 as well as parts of the hull were largely a French innovation. The cast APX-R turret featured a heavy cast cradle for the gun and a prominent domed cupola for the commander with vision slits. Although the commander had a seat inside the turret he normally stood. A flap at the back of the turret also dropped down to form a seat. The superstructure was also cast.

The rear-mounted engine provided power to the sprockets which drove the tracks around. The horizontal engine deck made it look similar to the H-38/39. The suspension comprised either side of a front drive sprocket, five road wheels and a low-mounted rear idler wheel. The road wheels were mounted in two articulated bogies, with two pairs and then a single one at the front. Movement of the wheels was cushioned by springs made up of horizontally-mounted rubber washers.

The hull was manufactured from three sections of rolled plate that were bolted together. The side plates carried the track bogies and the front the driving sprocket. The differentials and final drive were located under the cast nose plate.

Some R-35s were fitted with a special tail frame to assist the tank to cross wide trenches. Likewise others were modified to act as fascine carriers to assist crossing wide ditches or anti-tank trenches. These featured a girder framework designed to permit the fascine to be carried above the turret and delivered over the nose. Although the R-35 was France's most numerous light tank in 1940, its high fuel consumption greatly limited its range and it was outgunned by German tanks.

## R-40 (AMX-40)

Like the H-35, the R-35 was upgraded with the longer-barrelled 37mm SA 38 gun. This further development featured an entirely new vertical spring-type suspension with armoured skirting plates built by L'Atelier de Construction des Moulineaux (AMX). As a result this tank was known as the AMX-40 as well as the R-40.

The new suspension consisted of twelve small road wheels, with the drive sprocket at the front and the idler at the rear. There were also four track-return rollers. The small wheels and coil springs were covered by the side skirts, so it bore a passing resemblance to the Renault D2. This upgrade, referred to for convenience as the R-40, had superior cross-country performance than the earlier model. This was in part due to fitting tracks that were inspired by those on the Char B. Not many had been built by the outbreak of war and by 1940 only two battalions had been issued with the newer R-40.

By May 1940 there were 945 R-35/R-40 tanks in front-line service. The bulk of these some 810 were in support of French armies, their role being to support the infantry divisions, but their slow road speed gave them zero manoeuvrability. Another 135 were with General Charles De Gaulle's 4th Division Cuirassée de Réserve. Losses of the R-35 provided the Germans with ample photo opportunities.

## AMR 33 VM

French cavalry employed limited numbers of armoured cars during the First World War for reconnaissance purposes. They proved not very successful off-road so during the post-war period a number of requirements arose for various types of tracked reconnaissance vehicle to equip the cavalry. Amongst these was the Auto-Mitrailleuse de Reconnaissance (AMR) light tracked vehicle as well as the Auto-Mitrailleuse de Combat (AMC), a heavier support variant.

Built by Renault the AMR 33 VM light tank or tracked armoured car entered service in 1934–5. The hull was of riveted construction with the commander/gunner in the turret and the driver seated at the front to the left. The small turret, offset to the left, was armed with a single 7.5mm machine gun. The suspension looked slightly similar to British light tank designs, comprising four road wheels, with a twin bogie in the centre with single wheels next to the drive sprocket and the idler. At the top were four return rollers. It could manage about 37mph on the road and its tracks (rather than wheels) enabled it to cope with all types of terrain. The AMR 33 proved to be one of the most widely-used French light reconnaissance tanks and was issued to the French mechanized cavalry units.

## AMR 35 ZT

A second version known as the AMR 35 ZT was armed either with a 13.2mm machine gun or a 25mm anti-tank gun, although the first model had retained the 7.5mm machine gun. The heavier armament really put it in the AMC category. To keep the vehicle's weight down the armour, at 13mm, was no better than the AMR 33 and it had the same speed. The AMR 35 weighed some 6.5 tons compared to the 5 tons of the AMR 33. Just 200 AMR 35s were produced. The plan had been to replace this design with the H-35 but many were still in service in 1940.

## AMC 35 Type ACG1

An equally rare tank was the AMC 35 Type ACG1. Although this was also designed by Renault, it was built by AMX. This light tank is noteworthy because it was the first to feature a two-man turret. The AMC 35 employed a similar suspension to the R-35, but the hull and turret were a new design. It used bolted or riveted construction rather than cast. A Renault six-cylinder engine gave the tank a 25mph speed. Armament consisted of a 7.5mm machine gun and a 25mm or 47mm gun. Despite being a ground-breaking design, only 100 were ever built.

## FT-17

When the two-man Renault FT-17 light tank went into production in 1917 it was a milestone in tank design. In particular, it was the first tank to have a fully revolving turret, which provided all-round traverse for the tank's weapon. The first model to enter service in time to see action in 1918 was armed with an 8mm machine gun. The subsequent model which also saw combat was armed with a 37mm Puteaux gun. By the end of the war over 3,000 FT-17s had been built. It proved a huge export success and was widely copied.

By 1940 the FT-17 was completely obsolete. Crucially it was painfully slow, barely able to manage 5mph. This speed had been fine during the First World War when it only had to keep pace with advancing infantry, but was useless for modern mechanized warfare. During the 1920s the French made efforts to update the FT-17 which resulted in the FT-31. Despite its shortcomings when the Germans invaded France there were still around 1,600 in service. As a consequence, many were destroyed and even more were captured.

*Above*: The requirement to replace the First World War-vintage Renault FT-17 two-man light tank, seen here, resulted in the Renault R-35. Both would feature the same short 37mm gun.

*Opposite above*: This FT-17 captured in 1940 seems to be a source of some amusement to this German soldier and his friend with the camera. France's successor tanks used some of the same turret design features such as the domed cupola and rear access hatch.

*Opposite below*: Another abandoned FT-17 somewhere in France. Around 1,600 were in service when the Germans invaded France. The Germans were to deploy numbers of these tanks for security duties.

*Above*: Like the Hotchkiss H-35, the Renault R-35 appeared in the mid-1930s. Both looked very similar, using the same turret and scissor-type suspension. However, the R-35 had heavier armour and as a consequence was much slower, managing just 12mph on the road.

*Opposite above*: German soldiers examining the APX turret on an R-35. On this example the gun appears to have been removed from the cast cradle. The girder frame attached to the rear was intended to help the tank navigate wide trenches. The chains at the front indicate that it was under tow at some point until those involved gave up.

*Opposite below*: Intriguingly, another abandoned R-35 with its main armament removed. The driver gained access via the double hatch in the superstructure and glacis.

*Above*: German troops passing an R-35 that has lost both sets of tracks, exposing the drive sprockets. Its poor cross-country speed meant this tank type was mainly confined to paved roads when trying to deploy to the front.

*Opposite above*: This French commander managed to escape his R-35 via the turret hatch only to be killed outside the tank. This was a common fate for fleeing tank crew.

*Opposite below*: A German convoy passes a captured R-35. French tanks often had a two-tone camouflage paint scheme of sandy brown and olive green. The latter was sometimes bordered with a darker colour. There is no sign of any damage, suggesting the tank broke down.

*Above*: Insignia employing playing-card symbols were used by the French Army to identify sub-units. The turret clearly has a club painted on it. The missing left-hand engine access plate suggests mechanical trouble.

*Opposite above*: Renault exported the R-35 widely. This one is serving with the Yugoslav Army in 1940. The hull has been heavily camouflaged with the application of tree branches.

*Opposite below*: It is unclear what this R-35 is doing tilted on its side. However, it appears as if these German mechanics may have been trying to get the left-hand side track back on.

A captured Renault D-2. This tank had been replaced by the Char B1 but some were still in service in 1940 including with General Charles de Gaulle's newly-raised 4th DCR.

The FT-17 was cripplingly slow and could barely manage 5mph. Nonetheless this tank was built in very large numbers and was exported to numerous armies around the world. Initially it was armed with a Hotchkiss machine gun, but subsequent models replaced this with a 37mm Puteaux gun.

A quick snapshot to record the spoils of war – another obsolete Renault FT-17.

Not a tank wreck just yet – a camouflaged R-35 firing in the French Alps.

Another snapshot of a captured FT-17 – the main armament has been removed.

Although not a wreck, this is a rare shot of a camouflaged Renault AMR 33 VM light tank, which entered service in 1934. This two-man reconnaissance tank was armed with a 7.5mm machine gun and could manage 37mph on the road. Another version known as the AMR 35 ZT, armed with a 13.2mm Hotchkiss machine gun or a Hotchkiss 25mm anti-tank gun, was also produced.

Remains of an AMR 33 light tank caught on the streets. The side of the turret received a direct hit shattering the plate armour, which at its thickest was just 13mm.

# CHAPTER THREE

# French Heavies

The heavy B1 and S-35 tanks were used to equip France's newly-formed armoured and light mechanized divisions. Due to their size they were regularly photographed by the Wehrmacht.

## Char B1

The large and powerful Char de Bataille Renault B1 heavy tank provided the main striking power of the four Divisions Cuirassées or armoured divisions by 15 May 1940. The last division, created on that very day, was under the command of none other than General Charles de Gaulle. This in effect made it the most significant Allied tank of the Blitzkrieg era. Each division had four battalions of combat tanks, organized in a demi-brigade of two battalions of Char B1s and a demi-brigade of two battalions of lighter tanks, mainly Hotchkiss H-39s.

The requirement for the four-man Char B first originated in the early 1920s, though exact specifications were not agreed until 1926. Codenamed 'Tracteur 30', between 1929 and 1931 three prototypes were produced and trials with these resulted in the first production model, dubbed the Char B1, in 1935. The size and shape of the tank, with its long and high profile, showed the influence of the tanks developed during the First World War.

Nonetheless, in its favour it was well armed with a short-barrelled 75mm gun and a short 47mm gun as well as two machine guns. The APX turret was the same as that fitted on the Somua S-35. In addition it was well armoured for its time. The drawback with the 75mm gun was that it was mounted in the hull and could only be traversed by moving the tank. This was far from ideal under combat conditions and was an unwanted distraction for the driver. Gun elevation was limited to +25° and depression to -15°

The tank carried seventy-four high-explosive rounds for the 75mm and fifty armour-piercing and high explosive rounds for the 47mm gun, plus 5,100 rounds of machine-gun ammunition. Despite the Char B's size, a 250hp six-cylinder Renault engine gave a top speed of 17mph, which meant it could easily keep up with most of the French light tanks.

The tank was of box-like construction, with slab sides and suspension assemblies bolted to a girder frame and cross members. The driver sat in the front and also acted as gunner for the 75mm gun, which was yet another drawback. The gun was located to his right with air-blast gear designed to remove the toxic recoil fumes. Steering was by the Naeder hydrostatic type providing fine directional control through the tracks, which assisted in laying or sighting the gun. The gun sight was located not next to the weapon but below the driver's episcope.

The commander sat in the turret and operated the 47mm gun. The requirement for the two men tasked with controlling the tank, the commander and the driver, to act as gunners was a fundamental flaw in the Char B. The loader and radio operator were supposed to serve both the main guns. In addition, by German standards the one-man turret made the Char B unsuitable for front-line use.

## Char B1 bis

The first production model was followed by an upgraded version known as the Char B1 bis. It had an improved 47mm SA 35 turret gun that had a longer barrel than the SA 34 in the B1. This was housed in an enlarged APX 4 turret. The maximum armour on the B1 of 40mm was increased to 60mm on the bis. This could withstand any German anti-tank gun except for the famous dual-role 88mm Flak gun. The engine was also uprated to 300hp, which improved general performance and the speed very slightly. These improvements led to an increase in the overall weight from 28 tons to 32 tons.

## Char B1 ter

A third model known as the B1 ter with a 350hp diesel engine, improved side armour and limited independent traverse for the 75mm gun also appeared – but only five were ever built.

Production of the Char B was carried out by a series of French companies that included Renault, Schneider, FCM, FAMH (Saint Chamond) and AMX. Around 365 tanks were built, all of which were the improved B1 bis, except for 35-40 earlier B1. Some sixty-six B1 bis were with the 1st, 2nd, 3rd and 4th Division Cuirassées de Réserve and another fifty-seven with the independent companies. Numerous Char B1 bis fell into German hands in 1940 as did large quantities of other French tanks.

## D-2

The Renault Char D-2 medium infantry tank went into service in 1934. It was an improved version of the previous D-1 with a more powerful engine. It had a rear-mounted engine and a cast turret mounting a 47mm gun and a 7.5mm machine gun. It had up to 40mm of armour and its six-cylinder 150hp Renault engine gave a top speed of 15mph. The French Army, however, preferred the Somua medium tank and only around fifty D-2s entered service. Their slow speed and automotive unreliability meant that those at the front did not perform well against the panzers.

## S-35

The Char de Cavalerie Somua S-35 medium tank, which from a distance bore a passing resemblance to the Char B, is considered the best French tank of the Blitzkrieg era. Built by the Societé d'Outillage Méchanique et Usinage d'Artillerie or SOMUA at Saint Ouen, the S-35 first appeared in 1935. It was designed to equip the mechanized cavalry and was initially classified an Automitrailleuse de Combat but this was changed to Char de Cavalerie. It became one to the principal tanks of the DLMs or light mechanized divisions. Each of these had one regiment of S-35s and a regiment of H-39s in its tank brigade.

The S-35 had the same turret design as the Char B1 bis and the D-2, hence the similarity at a distance. However, it had few other similarities. The S-35 enjoyed a good road speed of 25mph without having to sacrifice armour protection. The latter was up to 55mm thick. Armament consisted of one 47mm gun and one 7.5mm machine gun mounted in an electrically-traversed turret. Such armament was as good or even better than that of the early panzers in 1940. One drawback though was that the tank commander also had to act as the gunner. Around 118 rounds of armour-piercing and high explosive were carried for the 47mm and 1,250 rounds for the machine gun.

The suspension was formed of nine small road wheels either side, two return rollers and a front idler. This was protected by side armour skirting. The S-35 was powered by a Somua V-8 engine with 190hp, that was linked to a synchromesh five-speed gearbox. This transmitted power to the tracks via rear drive sprockets. The driver and the radio operator, who were both seated in the front of the tank, gained access via door in the left-hand side of the hull. The S-35 weighed 44 tons compared to the 70 tons of the B1.

Although the S-35 was fast and reliable, and indeed better armed and armoured than its German opponents, the French simply did not have enough of them to make a difference to the outcome of the battle for France. Just 500 were built. The S-35 was more than a match for the early panzers, but poor tactics ensured they were not used to the best of their capability. Like all French tanks the one-man turret greatly impacted on its capability. Furthermore, weak points in the hull were created where the three cast sections were bolted together above the tracks. When these were hit by anti-tank fire it normally had a catastrophic effect.

## S-40

Production of an improved version of the S-35 commenced in 1940. The S-40 had a modified suspension and more powerful 220hp engine to improve cross-country performance. However, very few of these had been completed by May 1940. A self-propelled 75mm gun variant known as the SAu-40 was also in development but only got as far as a prototype.

## De Gaulle at Montcornet

The problem the French had, like the Soviets, was that they did not know how to get the best out of their tank force. Should they be massed in one place or dispersed? By the time they realized the Germans had opted for the former it was too late. Charles de Gaulle, who was a colonel at the time, had lobbied to get the French army to focus on concentrating its tank formations into an armoured fist. He even went as far as denouncing the French General Staff warning 'Your leaders are inept, and you are disarmed!'

As the battle for France raged on 15 May 1940 de Gaulle was promoted to the temporary rank of brigadier general. He was also given command of the new 4th DCR. Major General Doumenc handing over the division said 'Now is your chance, de Gaulle. You've believed a long while in the doctrines Germany is applying. Now use them!' What chance though did de Gaulle's tanks have when his division was only partially assembled and wholly untrained. Nevertheless he was sent to the front immediately.

De Gaulle resolutely attacked the Germans at Montcornet near Loan between 17–20 May. His job was to cover the withdrawal of General Touchon's 6th Army from the Maginot Line. He had defiantly declared 'to advance is the only way to force the enemy to retreat!' He received welcome reinforcements in the shape of Colonel Sudre's armoured demi-brigade, that included a battalion of tanks partially comprising Char B1 bis commanded by Major Bescond.

De Gaulle told Bescond 'I must have Montcornet. You are the champion of the B tanks: it is up to you to show what they are worth. Go and win your fifth stripe at Montcornet!' Although it was the strongest attack on the southern flank of the German breach, de Gaulle's unpreparedness and a lack of support helped thwart his operation.

The French air force was nowhere to be seen and the Luftwaffe's Stukas set about de Gaulle's forces as they prepared to attack. In the fighting that followed Major Bescon was killed and the 4th DCR was forced to fall back to Loan. De Gaulle lamented 'We were a forlorn hope nearly twenty miles beyond the Aisne; and we had to put an end to a situation that was perilous, to say the least.'

A few days later de Gaulle tried again, this time near Abbeville with a reinforced command including 150 tanks. Bravely he had unfurled his colours on the lead tank called 'Rhône' and headed the attack in person. Ultimately there was little he could do to delay the advance of two whole German armoured corps.

General Gamelin, the new French Commander-in-Chief, was impressed with de Gaulle's actions remarking he was 'an admirable, energetic and courageous leader'. On 2 June 1940 the 4th DCR was withdrawn from the battle. By this point France was all but lost. The German panzers had reached the Aisne and held Laon, just 70 miles from the French capital. On 5 June de Gaulle was appointed Under Secretary for War. It was, however, too late for him to put his ideas into practice. In the north the French and British armies were trapped and forced to escape via Dunkirk.

Elsewhere France's scattered divisions were decimated and destroyed in battle, the army retreating in almost complete disorder. For de Gaulle France's defeat was not just a military and political failure, it was also an intellectual one. The Germans had thought ahead and the French High Command had failed to keep pace. As a result, France's formidable tank forces were thrown away, having failed to save France. With Britain unable and unwilling to help after Dunkirk de Gaulle set about shipping as many French troops overseas as possible in order to carry on the fight. His tanks would not be going with them.

After the war General Georges was to observe:

The 4th DCR was improvised on the battlefield. Yet it was the only one that disorganized the German columns to a considerable extent when it was thrown against their flanks. So true is it that the DCRs must of necessity be commanded by bold, dynamic leaders who have reflected at length upon the potentialities of these special units in battle. Such was then the case with Colonel de Gaulle.

## German Spoils

After the humiliation of France's defeat, it had to suffer the indignity of having its own armour mustered in support of the German occupation. Germany deployed three independent tank battalions equipped with captured armour in France, the 100, 206 and 213. Abteilung (battalion) 100 was formed in April 1941 as an Ersatz und Ausbildungs (training and recruitment unit) at Schwetzingen in the Rhineland. The following year the battalion was stationed at Satory near Versailles and used to guard the railway. One detachment was also sent to Vercors in south-eastern France near Grenoble to counter the Maquis or French Resistance.

Ironically the battalion was sent to Normandy in May 1944 under Major Bardlenschlager. It deployed west of Carentan with its companies spread out in the area of Baupte, Carentan and Ste. Mere-Eglise. Abteilung 100 were tactically responsible to the 91st Airlanding Division and helped build anti-invasion defences. The battalion's order of battle by mid-1944 included some twenty-seven French tanks. On the morning of D-Day on 6 June 1944, the battalion went to battle readiness, but with no orders Bardlenschlager set out for the 91st's HQ at Houteville, never to be seen again.

The following day No. 1 Platoon 1st Company was sent towards St. Lo and No. 2 towards Carentan. Rapidly destroyed fighting the Americans, the battalion was finally reduced to an anti-tank company armed with panzerfausts and mounted on bicycles.

On 7 July 1944 the unit was officially disbanded – its French tanks long since scattered around the Normandy countryside like so much scrap.

The 100's sister battalion was the 206, formed as a reserve formation for the 7th Army at Satory in November 1941. By mid-January 1944 Panzer Abteilung 206 was equipped with fourteen Hotchkiss H-35, H-38 and H-39, four Somua S-35, which were issued to platoon and company commanders, five Renault B-1 bis some of which were flamethrowers, and two Hotchkiss training vehicles. By June 1944 it had sixteen Hotchkiss, two Somua, four Renault B-1 bis and two Renault R-35 tanks.

During D-Day the battalion was at Cap de la Hague on the northernmost tip of the Cotentin Peninsula and subordinate to the 243rd Infantry Division. Trapped along with the 243rd, 709th and 91st Divisions the 206 was completely annihilated during the Americans' battle for the Peninsula.

In 1941, as a result of Hitler's order to send armour to the Channel Islands, CinC West, Field Marshal von Witzleben, despatched twenty Renault FT-17/18 to Alderney, Guernsey and Jersey. When Abteilung 213 arrived the tanks were handed over to the infantry and used for airfield defence. By the end of 1944 only two were still serviceable, the rest having been cannibalized and used as airfield pillboxes. Also in 1941 a number of 47mm Pak 36(t) auf GW Renault R-35(f) self-propelled guns were sent to the Channel Islands. They were organized into special units and had nothing to do with the 213. By the end of 1942 there were twenty-two French self-propelled guns on Alderney, Guernsey, Jersey and Sark.

In September 1941 Hitler ordered heavier armour to be despatched. Rather than tie up vital panzers, a number of Char B1s were selected for the Channel Islands. Recruits were selected from 1st Panzer Ersatz Regiment at Erfurt and ended up at Foissy near Paris. There they formed Panzer Abteilung 213 equipped with Char B1s. The unit thought it was going to North Africa, but instead went to St. Malo and on to the Channel Islands. Arriving on Guernsey on 25 March 1942 the tanks were stationed at Tabor Chapel. Initially seventeen Char B1s went to Jersey and nineteen to Guernsey: of each batch twelve were normal PzKpfw Char B1 bis(f), while the other five were flamethrowers; the company HQ on Guernsey accounted for the additional two.

After the Allies landed in Normandy and with the capture of St. Malo on 15 August 1944 the Channel Islands were besieged. On 9 May 1945 Task Force 135 arrived to accept the garrison's surrender; the German infantry and tank crew were shipped off to England. Panzer Abteilung 213 is probably the only German armoured unit never to have fired a shot in anger.

Additionally, at least two German divisions in the West used French tanks. In October 1942 the 7th SS Freiwilllgen Gebirgs (Mountain) Division Prinz Eugen became operational and was equipped with Czechoslovakian, French, German and Italian surplus stocks. The division also had a battalion of tanks. By June 1943 a tank company was equipped with Hotchkiss H-39s, which were used in Yugoslavia in counter-insurgency operations against Tito's partisans.

The French Char B1 heavy tank was well armoured and well armed. However, the hull-mounted 75mm gun could only be traversed by moving the tank and the driver had to also act as the gunner. It first appeared in the mid-1930s and was built by a consortium of companies.

*Above*: The same tank head-on. This gives a clear view of the driver's position: the turret was slightly offset to the left hand side of the hull. The hull gun elevation was limited to +25° and -15°

*Opposite above*: The turret on the Char B1 was designed and built by APX. It was armed with a 47mm gun and a coaxial 7.5mm machine gun. The 47mm could fire both armour-piercing and high explosive rounds.

*Opposite below*: Another view of the same tank. The general shape of the hull was reminiscent of British First World War designs. Note the access hatch in the rear of the turret which was a common feature on French tanks.

The Char B1 was upgraded to produce the B1 bis, which was the most common variant. It had a more powerful engine, increased armour and a longer-barrelled 47mm gun. Crew access was on the right-hand side via a hatch in the hull. In common with most tank crews, the French liked to name their tanks – this example has been dubbed 'Tunis'.

The rear of this Char B1 shows how well its armour could stand up to enemy fire. There are almost a dozen strike marks.

'Vendee II' and its partner lost at the roadside. General Charles de Gaulle's counterattack at Montcornet and Abbeville involved Char B1s but they were pounded to a halt by the Luftwaffe and German artillery.

*Above:* This Char B1 was destroyed by a massive internal explosion that ripped open the hull and took off the turret. A second abandoned Char B1 lays just behind it. The large M and square turret recognition symbol indicate they belonged to the 4th DCR.

*Opposite above:* German troops gather around their prize. The elevation of the 75mm gun suggests the tank was being used in an indirect fire support role. Some seventy-four rounds of high explosive were carried for this weapon.

*Opposite below:* A German column passing abandoned Char B1s. The soldier in the middle of the road appears to be taking photographs.

*Above:* The Somua S-35 medium tank was the best France had to offer in 1940. It was more than a match for the panzers during the Battle for France, by which point 500 had been built.

*Opposite above:* From a distance the S-35 looked similar to the B1 because it used the same turret. However, it was almost half the weight of its heavy cousin. The hull was cast in three sections and bolted together above the tracks. This shot gives a clear view of the access doors on the left side of the hull, the rear drive sprocket, the air-intake grilles over the rear-mounted engine as well as the centrally mounted exhausts between the two grilles. The suspension has suffered damage as the side skirts are bent and buckled.

*Opposite below:* It is notable that many of the photos taken by the Germans tended to be of the rear of the S-35. The turret was armed with a 47mm SA 35 gun which had an elevation of +18° and a depression of -18° and a 7.5mm Model 31 coaxial machine gun. The later was mounted in an armoured shroud to the left of the main gun.

*Above*: The access hatches on the right-hand side of the S-35 were limited to just the engine compartment.

*Opposite above*: A German officer and a panzer commander pose on a stranded S-35. The French recognition roundel (red, white and blue) is painted on the turret hatch. There seems to have been no uniformity with the location of this symbol. Interestingly this tank appears to have the early APX I turret armed with the short 47mm gun.

*Opposite below*: The crew of this S-35 ended up getting their tank stranded in the middle of a river where they abandoned it, much to the amusement of German sightseers.

Some S-35s sported the French roundel on the turret hatch and the rear of the hull.

More abandoned S-35s. The French roundel on these has been applied to the rear of the turret opposite the hatch.

Another S-35 with the roundel on the rear of the hull.

Beside the R-35 the Char 2C looks absolutely enormous. A number of other European countries toyed with these massive breakthrough tank designs but quickly abandoned them as wholly impractical.

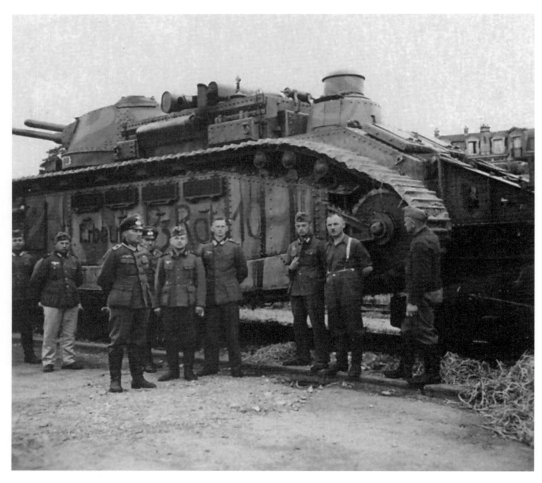

The enormous Char 2C heavy tank entered service with the French Army shortly after the end of the First World War. Armament consisted of a turret-mounted 75mm gun, but the 2C could only manage 4mph. Just ten were built and were serving with the 51st Tank Battalion in 1940 supporting the Maginot Line. They saw no action and most of them were pounced on by the Luftwaffe whilst being moved by train.

# CHAPTER FOUR

# Vickers Mk VI and Matilda

Britain's lack of tanks at the outbreak of war in 1939 was a glaring deficiency for the British Army. Those available were too lightly armoured and their guns were incapable of tackling Hitler's panzers on anything like equal terms. The famous Vickers Mk VI light tank and Matilda II infantry support tank constituted the most numerous British armour deployed to France in 1940. Consequently they became a source of great interest to the victorious Germans.

## Mk VIB

The Mk VI light tank series were numerically the most important armoured fighting vehicles of the British Army in 1939–40. Like its predecessors, the Mk VI was designed by Vickers-Armstrong Ltd and was chosen in 1935 along with other armoured fighting vehicles to be built by manufacturers outside the armaments industry to give companies experience in tank building. The Mk VIB was an improved version of the initial model and was built in far greater numbers.

In the same style as its predecessors the Mk VI's engine was installed on the right-hand side of the hull with the transmission led forward to the front drive sprockets. The driver was seated to the left and the turret housing the commander and gunner was also off set to the left. The tank used the Horstmann suspension which, while simple and dependable, did have a habit of shedding the tracks. Fortunately they could be replaced fairly easily. The suspension was formed by two, two-wheel bogie units on each side, that were sprung on twin coil springs, with the rear road wheel acting as the trailing idler. The Mk VIB was armed with a Vickers 0.303in machine gun and a Vickers 0.5in heavy machine gun, both water-cooled.

## Mk VIC

The subsequent Mk VIC was very similar, but lacked the large turret cupola and was armed with Besa 15mm and 7.92mm air-cooled machine guns. On both models the armour was just 14mm thick, meaning the Mk VI was only suitable for fast reconnaissance work. Even so, Mk VIBs were utilized by all the divisional cavalry regiments with the infantry divisions of the BEF. They were also employed as headquarters tanks with the 1st Tank Brigade.

In the British 1st Armoured Division Mk VICs formed a large proportion of its tank strength due to a delay in supplying the newer cruiser tanks. They were to prove no match for the panzers encountered in 1940. Although designed as a reconnaissance tank the Mk VI was often used in a cruiser role, its inadequate armour and armament invariably lead to heavy losses when facing anything heavier than a Panzer I. This tank type likewise served in the 1st Tank Brigade's headquarters.

## Matilda I

The heavier and earlier Matilda I (A11) Infantry Tank was first delivered to the British Army in 1936. It was a fine example of poor funding and inadequate design. Utilizing an underpowered lorry engine, initially the suspension kept shredding the tracks. The first batch of 60 were ordered in April 1937, later increasing to 140, all of which had been delivered by the summer of 1940. While the more numerous Matilda I's armour was almost impervious to the Germans' standard 37mm anti-tank guns, its Vickers machine gun lacked punch. Without an anti-tank gun, it simply could not take on the panzers.

## Matilda II

The lumbering British Matilda II infantry tank proved a nasty shock for the Germans at Arras in May 1940. Despite not being available in sufficient numbers, lacking adequate infantry and artillery support and no air cover, the tank's measure of success was largely due to its 78mm-thick frontal armour. This proved invulnerable to the German 37mm anti-tank gun.

The Matilda II was designed by Colonel Hudson's team at the Mechanisation Board in the mid-1930s, it benefited from work conducted on the A7 medium tank, which never came to fruition. In late 1937 an order for 165 Matilda IIs was placed. Disastrously, however, due to the shape and size of the armour castings the tank was not easy to mass-produce. This was to prove a major problem and two years later there were just two in service. Although heavily armoured – its frontal plating was more than twice that of the Panzer II and III – cross country it was slow and its 2-pounder (40mm) main armament lacked real penetrating power.

## Arras Counterattack

Within the British 1st Tank Brigade three battalions of the Royal Tank Regiment (RTR) were to be equipped with the Matilda II, consisting of the 4th at Farnborough, the 7th at Catterick and the 8th at Perham Down on Salisbury Plain. Unfortunately the only unit ready to be shipped to France was the 4th Battalion equipped with fifty Matilda I Infantry Tanks and seven MK VI light tanks. Production of the Matilda II remained grindingly slow and it was not until the eve of the German Blitzkrieg that the 1st Tank Brigade HQ and the 7RTR were shipped to France. Frustratingly 8RTR was not up to strength and was left behind, but 7RTR arrived on the continent with twenty-three Matilda IIs, twenty-seven Matilda Is and seven light tanks. The brigade commander Brigadier Douglas H Pratt was placed under the direct control of General the Viscount Gort, CinC BEF.

The 1st Tank Brigade was ordered to Tournai, but arriving at Enghein found the railway station bombed. The brigade gathered at Ath on 17 May 1940, only to be sent on a fool's errand in response to reports of a German breakthrough. Eventually reaching Orchies 16 miles south-east of Lille Brigadier Pratt joined a scratch force under Major General Frank Mason Macfarlane, Director of Military Intelligence at GHQ, dubbed 'Macforce'. British tanks were designed to cover just ten miles a day before maintenance; by the time they arrived back in Arras on 18 May they had travelled 120 miles. The following day General Erwin Rommel's 7th Panzer Division reached Cambrai just 24 miles south of Orchies.

Within a week of getting over the Meuse, seven German panzer divisions had pierced the French defences and on 20 May General Heinz Guderian's 19th Panzer Corps reached the Channel west of Abbeville. He then swept northward toward the ports of Boulogne, Calais and Dunkirk in an effort to cut off those British and French forces north of the River Somme. Early on the 20th 1st Tank Brigade and the 5th Division were ordered to the Vimy area north of Arras to reinforce the 50th Northumbrian Division. Placed under Major General Harold E. Franklyn, General Officer Commanding 5th Division, this force was known at 'Frankforce.'

The situation for the British was very desperate; the BEF had just four days' worth of supplies remaining and barely sufficient ammunition for another grapple with the Germans. The British tank force struggled along choked roads through Carvin and Lens to cover the 30 miles between Orchies and Vimy. The last of the brigade reached Vimy at 0500 hours on 21 May thereby delaying Franklyn's plans. The lack of the trains took its toll in wear and tear; from a total of seventy-seven Matilda Is nineteen had been lost and of the twenty-three Matilda IIs seven were unserviceable.

50th Division's commander, Major General Martel, was instructed to clear the south of Arras as far as the Cojeul River, a distance of just 10 miles. Following this the 5th Division's 13th Brigade was to advance south to link up with the 151st Brigade from 50th Division. These combined forces were to then push on to a line on the River Sensee to the south-east. In total Martel's attack force numbered some 3,500 troops supported by 74 tanks. He organized them into two mobile battle groups each consisting of a tank and infantry battalion supported by field artillery and anti-tank batteries. For the opening of the Arras attack the French 3rd DLM's S-35 tanks were to screen the British right flank.

The two British columns were to sweep south-east of Arras. The right-hand column, spearheaded by the 7RTR with twenty-three Matilda Is and nine Matilda IIs, was to push through Duisans, Walrus and Berneville to the Beaumetz-Arras highway, from where it was to attack toward Wailly, Ficheux and onto the Cojeul River. The left-hand column, lead by the 4RTR with thirty-five Matilda Is and seven Matilda IIs, was to drive through Dainville, Achicourt, then split clearing Agny to the south to Mercatel and the Cojeul; while just to the north the rest would attack through Beaurains, Neuville and then onto Wancourt on the Cojeul.

Facing them was Rommel's 7th Panzer Division consisting of Panzer Regiment 25 with about 180 tanks and the 7th Rifle Brigade numbering about 4,000 men. They were well supported by 105mm field guns and howitzers and 37mm anti-tank guns. Additionally the 23rd Flak Regiment included a battery of 88mm anti-aircraft guns, which could be used in an anti-tank role. Rommel easily out-gunned and outnumbered Martel's meagre attacking force.

At 1315 hours British tanks began moving the eight miles to their Arras-Doullens road start line without the infantry who had been delayed; they did not catch up until 1600 hours. Martel found that Maroeuil was already under shellfire at 1430 hours and that German troops were in Duisans to the south. The day did not start off well when British tanks accidentally engaged some French ones near the village. Luckily there were no losses before the error was realized.

Rommel found at Wailly that 'The enemy tank fire had created chaos and confusion among our troops in the village and they were jamming up the roads and yards with their vehicles, instead of going into action with every available weapon to fight off the oncoming enemy.' Moving west of Wailly, Rommel saw that the advancing British tanks, spearheaded by a Matilda II, had already crossed the Arras-Beaumetz railway and set about a Panzer III. British tanks were also pressing in from the north from Bac du Nord, which lay north-west of Wailly. Some of his infantry took flight, taking the crew of a howitzer battery with them.

The British though were taken by surprise by Rommel's well-concealed anti-tank guns and anti-aircraft guns positioned in the hollows and small woods. Rommel crept amongst the guns and personally assigned each its target. Some of his officers pointed out that the range was too great but Rommel knew they could not wait or they would be overrun. He then ordered a furious and rapid fire in an attempt to halt the oncoming Matildas. Despite being under fire themselves, Rommel's gun crews kept their nerve.

The British left-hand column got as far as Neuville and Wancourt before running into Rommel's screening defences. In the area of Tilloy-Beaurains-Agny the British overran the German's light anti-tank guns and some SS troops were put to flight. The British triumph was short-lived, as Rommel recalls: 'Finally, the divisional artillery and 88mm anti-aircraft batteries succeeded in bringing the enemy armour to a halt south of the line Beaurains-Agny.' The carnage amongst the British armour was considerable, according to Rommel: 'Twenty-eight enemy tanks were destroyed by the artillery alone, while the anti-aircraft guns accounted for one heavy and seven light [tanks].'

At 1900 hours Rommel ordered Panzer Regiment 25 to strike south-eastwards in order to take the British in the rear. South of Agnez, which lay west of Arras and Duisans respectively, the panzers ran into a superior force of British armour. In the following tank battle the Germans lost ten panzers (three Mk IVs, six Mk IIIs and a Mk I) but knocked out seven Matilda IIs and six anti-tank guns. They broke through and the British headed back toward Arras.

By 2215 hours the British left-hand column was withdrawing on Achicourt south of Arras, where the infantry conducted a hotly-contested rearguard action. On the right, six French tanks and two armoured personnel carriers got through to Warlus past midnight and covered the retreat. Ten Bren gun carriers covered the withdrawal of those men still at Duisans.

Belatedly the French 3rd DLM went into action on 23 May, only to be pounded to a halt by German dive-bombers and artillery. That evening the British abandoned Arras, withdrawing 18 miles north to the canal line running through La Bassee and Bethune, to Gravelines on the coast south-west of Dunkirk. Despite this retreat, the fighting at Arras enabled four British divisions and most of the French 1st Army to withdraw toward the coast.

## Matilda Losses

In total the British lost twenty-nine Matilda IIs in France. The Germans were understandably delighted to have Britain's heaviest armour fall into their hands for full technical exploitation. At Arras one of the Matilda IIs was discovered to have fourteen gouges where anti-tank rounds had failed to penetrate its thick armour. This meant when the Germans came up against the Matilda II in North Africa and on the Eastern Front they were already thoroughly familiar with its capabilities and how to defeat it.

*Above*: The British Mk VI light tank appeared in the late 1930s and saw combat not only in France but also North Africa. The Mk VIB was the final development of the Carden-Loyd series and was armed with one .50in and one .303in Vickers machine gun. It required a three-man crew: commander, gunner and driver. Like its French counterparts it could not stand up to the panzers or heavy gunfire.

*Opposite above*: The Mk VIC was armed with a BESA 15mm heavy machine gun with a distinctive long barrel and a coaxial 7.92mm BESA. This variant also dispensed with the turret cupola, instead employing two domed hatches to give access.

*Opposite below*: British Mk IVBs abandoned in France during the retreat of the BEF in 1940. On the road the VIB could manage a respectable 35mph or 25mph cross country, but its armour was just 14mm at its thickest.

*Above:* The A12 Matilda II infantry tank entered service in 1939 and was first employed by 7RTR during the retreat to Dunkirk.

*Opposite above:* Along with the Mk VI and the Matilda I, the Matilda II saw action at Arras on 21 May 1940 against Rommel's 7th Panzer Division. These two belonging to 7RTR were lost during the fighting at Arras. Both seem to have been ransacked judging by the debris strewn on the ground.

*Opposite below:* German troops inspecting a Matilda II. At Arras these tanks briefly ran amok before being halted by Rommel's gun line. Just under 3,000 had been built by the time production ceased in the summer of 1943. Very few though fought in the French campaign. Most ended up in North Africa and the Far East.

A blurred shot of another Matilda II lost in France. The Germans were able to glean valuable technical intelligence from the BEF's tanks, which meant the Afrika Korps were well equipped to deal with the Matilda when it arrived in North Africa.

*Opposite above:* Two Mk VIBs on the beach at Dunkirk. The BEF lost all its heavy equipment during the evacuation, including its tanks.

*Opposite below:* A Mk VIB lost at Dunkirk showing the armoured housing on the turret for the Vickers machine guns.

# CHAPTER FIVE

# Churchill

The British Churchill infantry support tank was first bloodied during the disastrous Dieppe raid in 1942, then in Tunisia and later in France on D-Day. After Dunkirk British Prime Minister Winston Churchill was left with fewer than 100 tanks for the defence of the mainland, so losses had to be swiftly replaced to repel Hitler's anticipated invasion. The Vauxhall company was asked to work on the A20 Infantry Tank, which was still in development, and to get it into production within a year. The A20 was a throwback to the First World War, intended to cope with heavily-shelled areas and obstacles such as wide trenches.

Originally the Belfast shipbuilders Harland and Wolff had been tasked to provide four mild steel prototype A20s, but the first of these showed that the design needed to be revised. A pilot model of the subsequent A22, Infantry Tank Mk IV, appeared in November 1940 and 500 were ordered, with the first 14 being delivered in mid-1941. Weighing in at 38 tons, it was by far the heaviest British tank in service.

Dubbed the Churchill in honour of the Prime Minister, the A22 was built by a production group of eleven manufacturers under the direction of Vauxhall. The hull was of composite construction with the outer armour bolted or riveted on. Notably it was the first British tank to have controlled differential steering, provided by the then new Merritt-Brown four-speed gearbox. With a crew of five it had a top speed of 17mph and a range of 100 miles.

In the best traditions of the British military, due to the dire situation this tank was understandably a rushed job. The engine was inaccessible, the petrol pump shaft tended to snap and the hydraulic tappets often broke, requiring an engine replacement. The list went on. Therefore, the early A22s required constant fine-tuning until all the bugs were ironed out, which earned the tank a bad reputation that stuck even after it had proved itself. During 1942–3 Vauxhall engineers on secondment became familiar faces with those units issued with the temperamental tank.

## Churchill I

Like so many British tanks the initial Churchill was woefully undergunned. The Mk I's armament consisted of a 2-pounder gun (with 150 rounds) and 7.92mm Besa machine gun mounted in a cast turret and a close support 3in howitzer (with fifty-eight rounds) in the front hull. The later was required because the 2-pounder could not fire high-explosive shells.

## Churchill II

This inability to fire HE was a major shortcoming especially in the Mk II, which was the same as the Mk I but with a 7.92mm Besa machine gun replacing the howitzer. These were issued to the newly-raised British tank brigades and the exiled Polish Army tank brigade. A few IIC were produced which featured the 2-pounder in the nose and the 3in howitzer in the turret. Both the Churchill I and II had exposed tracks and engine intake louvres on the hull sides that had side openings. Track covers and armoured front horns were fitted from May 1942. Likewise, the air intake was redesigned so that the opening was at the top to prevent engine flooding when wading.

## Churchill II Oke

In 1942 the Petroleum Warfare Department developed the Churchill Oke flamethrower tank. This comprised the Mk II with the Ronson flamethrowing system with a range of 40–50 yards, which had been designed for the tracked Universal Carrier. Once again this was a rushed job in order that the concept of a flamethrowing tank could be tested under combat conditions at Dieppe in the summer of 1942.

## Churchill III

In 1942 the Churchill Mk III appeared with a larger turret and up-gunned to a 6-pounder gun, the post-Dunkirk emergency requirements having meant that the ineffective 2-pounder had been kept in production long after it was obsolete.

## Churchill IV

As above but with a new cast turret. Apart from the turrets the Mk III and IV were identical.

## Churchill VI and VII

The Mk VI and VII were both armed with 75mm guns. The former was converted from the Mk IV. In contrast, the Churchill VII was a new mark with thicker integral armour (rather than the earlier composite construction), a new cast/welded turret with cupola and circular instead of square hull side escape doors. Both were used in the North-west Europe campaign of 1944–5.

## Churchill V and VIII

The Mk V and VIII were armed with a 95mm howitzer. These were essentially rearmed Churchill IVs and VIIIs respectively.

## Canadian Churchills

The Canadian 14th Tank Battalion (The Calgary Tank Regiment) had been mobilized on 11 February 1941 and by 20 June was on its way to Britain. Initially the Calgarys were equipped with British Matilda II tanks for training purposes. By the end of the month the battalion had thirteen Churchill tanks, but it was still equipped with twenty-nine Matildas. An inkling of the unit's role in the Dieppe attack was gained on 4 December 1941 when their diary notes:

> A special film called 'Combined Operations' was shown to Officers and NCOs in the 'A' Sqn NAAFI hut. This film showed the various types of landing craft built for assaulting a hostile coast, and also the various ways in which such a coast may be attacked.

On 16 August 1942 the Calgarys, now the 14th Tank Regiment, transported eighteen Churchill tanks from Seaford to Gosport ready for embarkation. The rest moved to Newhaven under their own power. The following day they were loaded onto the landing ships, by 0300 hours on the 19th they were eight miles off Dieppe. The tanks were to attack in four waves; the first with nine tanks supporting the assaulting infantry; the second with twelve tanks; the third with sixteen tanks and the fourth with the rest of the regiment. Following a preliminary bombardment, the landings started at 0530, though a naval engagement in the Channel followed by air attacks tipped the defenders off that something was going on. During the run in to Dieppe the Tank Landing Craft (LCTs) were 15 vital minutes, late leaving the infantry pinned down on the beach.

The German defences at Dieppe were such that the Churchills were hemmed in and could not penetrate the town, where they could have created havoc. From a force of twenty-nine tanks landed during Operation Jubilee, two sank and twelve never got off the beach. Although the remaining fifteen got onto the esplanade, they could not penetrate the German anti-tank obstacles. When the smoke had cleared the Germans salvaged six Churchill Mk Is, seven Mk IIs and ten Mk IIIs. Most of these were badly damaged but one of each type was sent to the German Army Weapons Office at Kummersdorf for technical exploitation.

Following Dieppe, the German Captured Tank Company 81 found itself the recipient of some of the repaired Churchill IIIs. At the end of the year the unit became Panzer Regiment 100 and two of the Churchills remained in service until the close of 1943. That year one of the tanks was photographed aboard a train at the Yvetot railroad yards. They were then passed on to Captured Tank Unit 205, where they ended up being used for target practice due to a lack of spares and ammunition.

Britain sent some Churchill Mk I, II and IIIs to Russia and three Mk IIIs fought at El Alamein with the 8th Army. However, the Germans next properly came up against the Churchill tank in Tunisia where it served with the British 1st Army, most notably with the 142nd Royal Tank Regiment at the Battle of Medjez el-Bab in March 1943. Production was to have stopped but its success in Tunisia meant it continued to be built and was employed in the Italian campaign.

## Churchill 'Funnies'

In various guises the Churchill was later to play a highly specialized engineering role in the D-Day landings on 6 June 1944. The Allied assault on Germany's Festung Europa, or Fortress Europe, in June 1944 saw British military ingenuity at its best, resulting in a unique armoured formation. From its creation in 1942 the 79th Armoured Division was a regular armoured unit, but the following year, with the impending invasion of German-occupied France, it was earmarked for a key role. British military authorities, having learned a sharp lesson after the disastrous Dieppe raid, realized it was vital to have specialized armoured fighting vehicles that could punch through the hard crust of the Germans' Atlantic Wall defences. The 79th was allocated this tough task.

Dubbed 'The Funnies', the division was equipped with specialized AFVs. Amongst these the Armoured Vehicle Royal Engineers (AVRE) consisted of various developments mounted on the Churchill tank chassis. Churchill Mk III and IVs were equipped with a 290mm Petard spigot mortar for bunker-busting. Some of these, nicknamed the 'Bobbin', were fitted with a carpet layer for crossing soft ground. Other variants of the AVRE included the ARK (Armoured Ramp carrier), the mine-clearing Bullshorn Plough and the SBG (Small Box Girder) Assault Bridge. These vehicles were operated by the 5th and 6th Assault Regiments Royal Engineers (ARE).

Another key specialized Churchill was the Crocodile. This flamethrower variant used the Mk VIII. The flame projector was fitted in place of the hull machine gun. The flame fuel was carried in a trailer with the fuel being pumped under the belly of the tank. The flamethrower had a range of up to 120 yards firing eighty one-second bursts. This type arrived in Normandy just after D-Day.

## Black Prince

A 'Super Churchill' variant armed with the powerful 17-pounder gun, known as the Black Prince, was developed, though it never went into production. Nonetheless, by the end of the war 5,640 Churchills had been built.

Built in 1941, the Churchill Mk I's turret armament consisted of a 2-pounder and 7.92mm Besa machine gun, with a close support 3in howitzer in the front hull.

The Mk II was the same as the Mk I but with a 7.92mm Besa machine gun replacing the hull howitzer.

*Above:* The Churchill III, seen here, went into service in March 1942 and was the first to mount the 6-pounder gun. Mk I, II and IIIs were all involved in the Dieppe raid on 18 August 1942, serving with the Canadian Calgary Tank Regiment.

*Opposite above:* Wreckage of a Canadian Churchill I at Dieppe. It is identifiable by the 3in howitzer in the front of the hull. On the Mk II the later was replaced by a machine gun. Both models featured a cast turret armed with a 2-pounder gun and a coaxial machine gun.

*Opposite below:* A burning Churchill III stuck on the shingle on Dieppe beach. After the raid was thwarted the Germans salvaged ten Mk IIIs as well as six Mk Is and seven Mk IIs.

Am Strand von Dieppe! 19.8.42

*Above*: German troops examining a Churchill tank tantalisingly within sight of Dieppe. The rounded cast turret indicates this is a Mk I or II. Initially, because of the use of tanks, the Germans were not sure if the attack at Dieppe heralded a full-blown invasion or if it was just probing their defences.

*Opposite above*: Another view of the same Mk III, its landing craft ablaze behind it. The tanks were unable to get off the beach to support the Canadian infantry and British Commandos.

*Opposite below*: This long shot shows four Churchills stranded at Dieppe, with two on the beach and two in the sea. The Canadians committed about sixty Churchills to the assault with two-thirds of them landing with the first three waves.

*Above:* The Churchill VI and VII were armed with a British-built version of the American 75mm gun. This is the Mk VI as it has the square escape doors on the side of the hull, which were circular on the Mk VII.

*Opposite above:* Stranded Canadian Churchill III called 'Betty'. The tank seems to have shed its left-hand track. The pipes at the back were an exhaust extension designed to help the Churchills wade ashore.

*Opposite below:* The Churchill was later used in North Africa, Italy and again in France supporting D-Day. The AVRE or Armoured Vehicle Royal Engineers variant was armed with a massive 290mm spigot mortar. Some 180 Mk IIIs were converted to this AVRE role by 6 June 1944, which equipped the 1st Assault Brigade of the 79th Armoured Division.

*Above*: A Churchill VII. Both the Mk VI and VII models supported the British infantry divisions during the North-west Europe campaign of 1944–5. They were backed by the Churchill V and VIII which were both armed with a 95mm howitzer.

*Opposite above*: Front of the Churchill VII showing the driver's vision port and the hull machine-gun mounting.

*Opposite below*: A preserved Churchill VII outside the D-Day museum in Portsmouth. This was a redesigned version of the earlier models and saw action in the North-west Europe campaign of 1944–5.

# CHAPTER SIX

# Sherman

The world-famous American M4 Sherman first came into service in 1942. As the most numerous of Allied tank types it was involved in all the major battles from D-Day, Arnhem, the Ardennes and on to the Elbe. The M4 medium tank was easily the most common tank of the whole of the Second World War, with over 40,000 produced. It was a straightforward design that was easy to manufacture and was adaptable to numerous other roles such as self-propelled gun and tank destroyer. The General Sherman or Sherman for short was actually a British name that became popular with all other users including the Americans.

## Sherman M4/M4A1-A4

Design of the M4 as a 75mm gun-armed medium tank started in early 1941 and was intended to replace the stopgap M3. The latter was flawed by its main armament being mounted in the hull, but many of the other elements of the M3 such as the power pack, transmission and suspension design had proved efficient and were adopted.

On the Sherman the 75mm was mounted in a fully rotating turret. The prototype was completed by September 1941 and after some tinkering the M4 went into production the following year. The Sherman was employed by the American and British armies on almost every front from 1942 onwards.

Ensuring adequate engine supplies meant different versions of the Sherman employed different engines. Most notably the Wright engine was used in the M4 with welded hull, M4A1 was the M4 but with a cast hull, the General Motors 6046 twelve-cylinder diesel engine was used in the M4A2, the Ford GAA V-8 petrol engine in the M4A3 and the Chrysler A57 thirty-cylinder petrol engine in the M4A4 (longer hull). These were dubbed the Sherman I to V respectively by the British Army.

Space simply does not permit an extensive survey of all the different Sherman production models and the array of special-purpose variants. The basic shape of the hull included a well-sloped glacis plate, though construction varied with the A1 rounded cast hull being the closest to the original design. The M4, although the first in designation, was the third type to enter service, featured an all-welded hull as did the A2, A3 and A4. The combinations though did vary enormously.

The Sherman started life armed with a 75mm M3 gun with a coaxial 0.30in Browning machine gun. A second machine gun was fitted in a ball mounting in the front of the hull. Changes to the armament during production included replacing the 75mm gun with a 76mm or 105mm.

On the Western Front Hitler's panzers were overwhelmed by the M4 Sherman. By 1944 tank production had been switched to armoured cars, half-tracks, self-propelled artillery and tank killer vehicles. Also earlier versions of light and medium tanks were refurbished. At the end of 1944, in the wake of the D-Day landings, Operation Market-Garden and the Battle of the Bulge demand for tanks began to increase again. Between 1940 and 1945 America rolled out almost 89,000 tanks. The principal Sherman variant in 1945 was the M4A3.

The most common Allied tank to fight in Normandy was the M4 and M4A1 Sherman. Mechanically reliable, it was however handicapped by thin armour and a gun lacking sufficient punch. Its good cross-country speed and higher rate of fire could not make up for these two key shortcomings. Tank crew survival was paramount: tanks could be replaced relatively easily but not experienced crews. The Sherman had a nasty habit of burning when hit and if this happened the crew only had a 50 per cent chance of survival.

Two-thirds of the tanks used by British, Canadian and Polish armoured units in Normandy were Shermans, the rest being mainly British-built Cromwells and Churchills. The Cromwell cruiser tank was numerically and qualitatively the most significant British tank and along with the Sherman formed the main strength of the British armoured divisions. However, even armed with a 75mm gun it was inferior to the late-model Panzer IVs and the Panther. Although fast, the narrowness of the hull made upgunning it very difficult.

## Sherman Crab

Designed to clear minefields and barbed wire, the British Sherman Crab was produced to support the British and Canadian landings at Gold, Juno and Sword Beaches on D-Day. It consisted of a Sherman V (M4A4) gun tank fitted with a rotating flail, driven by the main drive shaft, with an effective depth of about 5in. Three regiments of the 79th Armoured Division were equipped with Crabs, the 22nd Dragoons, 1st Lothian and Border Yeomanry and the Westminster Dragoons.

## Sherman DD

The British amphibious Sherman Duplex Drive (DD) was also developed to support the D-Day landings. In order to provide the vanguard assault forces with sufficient armour support, swimming tanks were required. The DD tank was fitted with steel decking around the hull, upon which a screen could be raised by thirty-six air tubes and secured by hinged struts. The front screen could be lowered to facilitate firing.

Propelled by twin screws, hence duplex drive, the tank could swim at 4–5 knots. Three regiments of the 79th Armoured Division were equipped with DD tanks, the 4th/7th Royal Dragoon Guards, the 13th/18th Hussars and the 1st East Riding Yeomanry. Three US tank battalions were also equipped with the DD tank which were deployed in support of the landings at Omaha and Utah Beaches.

## Sherman Firefly

Some of those Shermans supplied to Britain were modified to take the British 17-pounder gun. These were dubbed the Firefly and issued in 1944 for the Normandy campaign. Unfortunately, due to the delayed Challenger tank programme a shortage of 17-pounders meant that Fireflies were only issued one per Sherman troop. Larger numbers were not available until early 1945.

The Germans soon realized that the larger gun in the Sherman Firefly constituted the biggest threat, as a resulted they tended to be targeted first by the panzers. The artist Rex Whistler, who was serving with the British Guards Armoured Division, came up with a disruptive paint pattern that was designed to disguise the length of the 17-pounder barrel. By painting the last half of the barrel in a lighter colour it was intended to make it look like the regular 75mm gun from a distance.

## M10 and M36

To compensate for not producing a successor tank soon enough, the Americans developed tank destroyers based on the Sherman with guns that could penetrate at least 80mm of armour at 1,000 yards. Notably the M10 was armed with a 3in gun and the M36 was armed with a 90mm gun, though these were never available in sufficient numbers. They were introduced into service in 1943 and 1944 respectively. The 3in gun was intended to tackle the Tiger, but being only able to penetrate the frontal armour at 50 yards rendered it all but ineffective against it. Those Sherman based M10s issued to British units were designated the Wolverine. These were upgunned in late 1944 with the 17-pounder gun to produce what was called the Achilles.

## Late-War Entries

Late-war American tank entries included the M24 Chaffee light tank armed with a 75mm that came into service in 1944; three types of Motor Gun Carriage, the M19, M37 and M41 were built using the same chassis but very few saw action before the end of the Second World War. Between April 1944 and June 1945 over 4,000 Chaffees were built and they went on to give notable post-war service. The American M26 General Pershing heavy tank, armed with a 90mm gun, was produced largely too late to see action, although a few saw combat at Remagen in Germany and some were used in the Pacific.

*Above:* A Sherman edges past a burning comrade in Normandy in 1944. The tank commander always had to be wary of ambush in such situations. To assist the driver, the commander's head is poking out between the open turret hatches, which attracted the added danger of sniper fire.

*Opposite above:* The Sherman M4 series medium tank was the most common Allied tank of the Second World War: consequently, it was the most photographed. A column of British Shermans in Normandy in 1944. The fourth tank back is a Sherman Firefly. Throughout the war the Sherman had to rely on the skill of its crew and weight of numbers to prevail over the superior panzer designs. Large numbers were destroyed and damaged during the fighting in Normandy.

*Opposite below:* The Sherman variants with petrol engines had a nasty habit of burning when hit, as these two lost in Normandy testify. The rubber tyres on the road wheels were destroyed in the blaze.

An infantryman hurries past the same tank. The open turret hatch indicates that the crew have bailed out. They normally had a 50:50 chance of survival if hit. Most crewmen preferred to take the chance of being mown down by gunfire than burn.

This American Sherman and German assault gun outside Carentan are horribly close. The Sherman is still smouldering. The road wheel tyres have gone and the turret shows signs of scorching.

The armour on the Sherman could only take so much punishment. At its thickest the armour was 75mm and at its thinnest 12mm.

*Above:* Another burnt-out Sherman left at the roadside.

*Opposite above:* The fighting at Villers-Bocage on 13 June 1944 resulted in a bloody nose for the 7th Armoured Division. This welded-hull Sherman lays derelict in the streets. The turret has been penetrated just to the left of the gun mantlet. The Desert Rats' divisional symbol is just visible above the 76.

*Opposite below:* The Sherman had a very distinctive suspension, comprising six road wheels in pairs either side attached to three armoured spring units, with the drive sprocket at the front and idler wheel to the rear. If hit the road wheels were easily damaged. The four wheels on these two bogies have almost been shot to pieces.

*Above*: Burnt-out M10 amongst the Normandy hedgerows.

*Opposite above*: The British up-gunned some of their M4A1 (Sherman II), M4A3 (Sherman IV) and M4A4 (Sherman V) with the 17-pounder gun to create the Sherman IIC Firefly, Sherman IVC Firefly and Sherman VC Firefly respectively. The latter was the most common variant – seeing combat in Normandy and North-west Europe. The long barrel tended to mean the Firefly got targeted first by German gunners.

*Opposite below*: A Sherman-based M10 tank destroyer abandoned on the streets of a Norman town. Either the crew or supporting infantry were caught in the open by enemy fire, as the body and scattered personal equipment at the back of the vehicle show.

A Sherman in Normandy being rescued by two armoured recovery vehicles based on the M3 chassis.

This example supporting US infantry in a Belgian town is a M4A3. The prong on the nose is a Culin hedgerow cutter developed for use in Normandy. Tanks fitted with such breaching devices were dubbed 'Rhinos'.

From the shape of the turret this is an M4A2 or M4A3 armed with the 76mm gun. It appears to have taken a direct hit in the engine compartment then burned.

This Sherman was captured by the Germans and pressed into service for their Ardennes offensive. It was recaptured on 24 January 1945. Photographic evidence shows that the Germans also made use of both the 76mm and 17-pounder Shermans.

Late-production Canadian Sexton self-propelled guns used M4 bogies with trailing return rollers, rather than the M3-type bogies on the initial version. The Sexton was similar to the American M7 Priest but armed with the British 25-pounder rather than the US 105mm howitzer. Although this example has the M4 suspension, it has the earlier three-piece nose, which was replaced by a one-piece cast nose. Armoured self-propelled guns such as this helped reduce the damage caused by German counter-battery fire. However, the open fighting compartment left the gunners exposed.

Shermans belonging to the Guards Armoured Division lost during the start of Operation Market-Garden on 17 September 1944.

Wreckage of an M18 tank destroyer lost during the Battle of the Bulge in the winter of 1944–5. Unofficially it was known as the Hellcat. Armed with a 76mm gun, thanks to its power-to-weight ratio it was considered one of the best tank destroyers of the Second World War.

M10 tank destroyer knocked out during the Battle of the Bulge.

A Sherman of the US 741st Tank Battalion caught on the streets of Leipzig in 1945. While supporting the US 2nd Infantry Division in securing the city the entire crew were killed, one of whom lies covered-up in front of the burning tank. For obvious reasons tankers hated fighting in cities and other built-up areas.

# CHAPTER SEVEN

# Panzer I, II and III

At the time of the invasion of France in 1940, the Panzer I, II and III were Hitler's most numerous panzer types. They rapidly proved to be under-armed and under-armoured and by 1943 were obsolete, being replaced by the Panzer IV, Panther and Tiger. The latter became the poster boys of the fighting during 1944–5.

## Panzer I

In the early 1930s when it was illicitly decided to expand and re-equip the German armed forces, a requirement arose for a training tank. Daimler-Benz, Henschel, Krupp, MAN and Rheinmetall were all asked to prepare prototypes similar to the British Vickers-Carden-Loyd light tank. The Krupp design designated LKAI was chosen for a production model which became the Panzer IA. A second prototype, LKBI, which had a more powerful engine, became the Panzer IB.

The early versions of both models had open-topped hulls and no turrets. These were dubbed landwirtschaftliche Schlepper (Las.S – or agricultural tractor); this was to hide the fact that Germany was planning to build a tank force that had been forbidden under the terms of the Versailles Treaty. The arrangement of both models was the same, with a rear-mounted engine and transmission forward to the front drive sprockets.

The crew compartment was in the centre with the driver to the left. The turret was offset to the right and was armed with two machine guns. The front road wheel on the suspension was sprung independently on a coil spring with the remaining wheels in pairs on leaf springs linked by a girder.

On the Panzer IB the larger engine required a lengthened hull which necessitated an extra road wheel either side. About 500 IAs were built, while some 2,000 IBs were ordered. They were tested in Spain and then saw action during the invasion of Poland and France. Their thin armour inevitably meant that large numbers were knocked out and as a result were photographed.

## Panzer II

Although the German army instigated a programme to produce medium tanks armed with guns capable of firing both high-explosive and armour-piercing rounds, this proved a slow process. As an interim measure it was decided to build a 10-ton light tank to supplement the 6-ton Panzer I. It was proposed that the Panzer II would take a three-man crew and be armed with a 20mm cannon. Prototypes were made by Henschel, Krupp and MAN in the mid-1930s. The MAN design was chosen for production.

The first to appear was the Panzer II Ausf a1 followed by small numbers of the a2, a3 and b. These early models had a suspension similar to that of the Panzer I. However, the Ausf c had an entirely new type of suspension and a much more powerful engine, which featured in subsequent models. Like its predecessors, the Ausf c had a rear-mounted engine with transmission through front mounted drive sprockets. The suspension comprised five medium-sized road wheels either side each sprung on leaf springs. Blooded in Poland, the German army had 955 Panzer IIs at the start of the campaign in the West.

## Panzer III

The German Army in the 1930s came up with two requirements for a 15-ton tank armed with a 37mm or 50mm anti-tank gun and a 20-ton medium tank armed with a 75mm support gun. Prototypes of the former were ordered from Daimler-Benz, Krupp, MAN and Rheinmetall. These were tested in the late 1930s with the Daimler-Benz model being picked for development.

The early models, Ausf A, B, C and D, had differing types of suspension but the hull and turret was largely the same. The suspension was not standardized until the Ausf E, which consisted of six road wheels either side using a transverse torsion bar suspension system. Three return rollers either side supported the upper run of the tracks.

The Ausf E was fitted with the more powerful Maybach twelve-cylinder engine, the HL 120 TR. This generated 300hp compared to the 250hp of the earlier versions. The engine was installed in the rear of the hull with the power transmitted to the front-mounted driving sprockets. The turret was mounted centrally and armed with a 37mm gun. General Heinz Guderian had wanted a 50mm gun but this was not ready in time. The bigger gun was subsequently mounted in later models after the French campaign and these variants saw action on the Eastern Front and in North Africa. Coaxial armament comprised an MG 34 machine gun with another one mounted beside the driver in the front of the hull.

The early models, including some Ausf E, saw action in Poland and France. By 1944 the Panzer III had been all but phased out of front-line service on the Western Front and was mainly retained for specialized functions such as command and recovery tanks. As a result most Panzer III wrecks on the Western Front were photographed in 1940.

A Panzer I Ausf B knocked out in France during 1940. This two-man tank was thinly armoured and only armed with machine guns. The B model had a more powerful engine than its predecessor, which necessitated a longer hull with an extra road wheel and extra return roller.

The same Panzer I Ausf B wreck photographed from the side. Judging by the debris it was thoroughly ransacked by whoever destroyed it.

*Above:* What appears to be a burning Panzer I. This light tank only had a maximum of 13mm of armour and was vulnerable to any light gun. Many Panzer Is were destroyed by the British 2-pounder anti-tank gun during the retreat to Dunkirk.

*Opposite above:* Likewise the Panzer II, with just 30mm of armour, was also vulnerable to British and French anti-tank gun fire in 1940. This one has burnt out, a common problem with tanks powered by petrol engines.

*Opposite below:* Another burnt-out Panzer II – production was soon shifted over to using the chassis as a self-propelled gun mount.

Wrecked early model Panzer III Ausf D – this type saw combat in Poland and Norway. However, this one lacks the Polish campaign recognition symbol and the countryside looks more in keeping with France.

Remains of a snow-covered Panzer II.

# CHAPTER EIGHT

# **Panzer IV**

The fourth and most enduring of the German tank types was the Panzer IV. Throughout the war on the Western Front it provided the backbone of the Panzerwaffe. It also bore the brunt of the fighting and as a result thousands were knocked out. Some 8,500 were manufactured.

This tank arose from a requirement for a 20-ton medium support tank armed with a short 75mm gun capable of firing high-explosive shells. In the late 1930s Krupp won the contract to develop a production model. The suspension featured eight road wheels on each side suspended in pairs on leaf springs. The drive sprockets were at the front and the tracks were carried forward from the idler on four return rollers either side. The rear idler wheels were raised off the ground. The eight road wheels and four return rollers made it easy to identify from the Panzer III which had a six-and-three combination suspension either side.

The rear mounted engine was the same as that used in the Panzer III from the Ausf E onwards – the twelve-cylinder Maybach HL 108TR. Cooling was achieved by drawing air into the hull on the right-hand side, which was them passed through the radiator and out through grilles on the left-hand side. Power was passed forwards through a dry plate clutch and gearbox to the drive sprockets. The gearbox in the Ausf A had five forward speeds which in the Ausf B was boosted to six. Engine power was also boosted with the larger HL 120TR.

All the early models of the Panzer IV looked externally alike with the short-barrelled 75mm L/24 gun. This changed with the later Ausf F2 with the introduction of the long-barrelled 75mm. All had a coaxial machine gun. From the Ausf G the long-barrelled gun was standard.

The Ausf A had 14.5mm of armour on the hull and 20mm on the turret. On the Ausf B–D the frontal armour was increased to 30mm. As a result of experience in Poland, armour on the hull was increased to 40mm on the hull sides and 60mm at the front. Some 278 Panzer IVs of all types were available at the beginning of the campaign in the West in 1940. However, once deployed to Russia the early-model Panzer IVs were found to be only capable of tackling the Russian T-34 from behind.

The Ausf G and H appeared in 1942 and 1943 respectively. The latter proved to be the most produced version. Both drew on the F2 interim model and were armed with the long-barrelled 75mm L/48 gun. The last model, the Ausf J, was similar but incorporated some changes to speed up production. Most notable was the deletion of the power traverse in the turret, leaving just the two-speed hand traverse system. This was understandably unpopular with the gunner and loader. The omission though also made space for a greater fuel capacity to give the tank extra range.

The most common types of panzer in Normandy in 1944, totalling 748 tanks, were the Panzer IV Ausf H and Ausf J, which went into production in 1943 and 1944 respectively. With frontal armour of 80mm and a 75mm KwK 40 L/48 anti-tank gun they provided the mainstay of the German panzer divisions. The gun had a 20 per cent greater muzzle velocity than that of the American built M4 Sherman's 75mm gun, meaning it could punch through 92mm of armour at 500 yards, while the Sherman could only manage 68mm.

Normally the Panzer IV was allocated to the II Abteilung or 2nd Battalion of a panzer regiment, although there were a number of exceptions. In Normandy the I Abteilung of the 9th Panzer Division's Panzer Regiment 33 was equipped with Panzer IVs and both Abteilung of 21st Panzer's Panzer Regiment 22 were equipped with it. During 1944–5 destroyed and abandoned Panzer IVs were regularly photographed by the triumphant Allies.

Early model Panzer IV Ausf E being recovered from a ditch. This type saw action in France in 1940 and elsewhere before being phased out in 1944. From the Ausf F2 onwards it was armed with a long-barrelled 75mm gun.

This Panzer IV Ausf D has either been damaged or is undergoing maintenance. The early model Panzer IVs, armed with the short-barrelled 75mm gun, saw action during the invasion of France in 1940.

A burnt-out Panzer IV somewhere in northern France. Almost 750 Panzer IVs were committed to the Battle of Normandy, and nearly every single one of them was lost. The banks of the Seine in the Rouen area became a graveyard for any armour that had survived because all the bridges were down.

Two Panzer IV Ausf Js from the 2nd SS Panzer Division. These tanks were lost to the US 30th Infantry Division at St Fromond east of the road from Carentan to St Lô on 9 July 1944. The tank nearest the camera has lost almost all its side skirts.

A Panzer IV Ausf H serving with the 21st Panzer Division in Normandy on 1944. It was knocked out to the north-east of Caen while fight from a hull-down position. It suffered a direct hit to the front of the turret. A neighbouring Panzer IV received a direct hit on the side of its turret, indicating they were outflanked.

Another Ausf H, this time belonging to the 2nd Panzer Division, also lost in Normandy. It is covered in rubble, including bricks from a nearby house.

An impressive sight. A Panzer IV and Panther graveyard near Isigny-sur-Mer in Normandy. The tanks are believed to have come from the Panzer Lehr Division along with the 2nd and 2nd SS Panzer Divisions. The US Army gathered them up from the surrounding countryside for safe disposal – ammunition and booby traps had to be removed. After the war in the late 1940s all the vehicles were sold off as scrap. Sadly, few if any of them ever got as far as a museum.

*Above*: Remains of the last version of the Panzer IV, the Ausf J. This was knocked out in January 1945. The 75mm gun has lost its muzzle brake.

*Opposite above*: The Isigny-sur-Mer tank graveyard photographed from a different angle. At least five Panzer IVs are visible behind the Panther in the foreground.

*Opposite below*: This Panzer IV would have needed an armoured recovery vehicle or a heavy duty half-track to recover it from this predicament.

Another Ausf J, abandoned in Belgium.

A Panzer IV destroyed by Allied fighter-bombers during Hitler's last-ditch Ardennes offensive. From then on the panzers on the Western Front were conducting a fighting retreat.

# CHAPTER NINE

# **Panther**

The Panzer V or Panther was built as Germany's answer to the T-34. After the Panzer IV it was the most numerous panzer on the Western Front and was again photographed a lot during the Normandy and Ardennes battles. Almost 6,000 Panthers were built between 1943 and 1945.

The Panther represented the pinnacle of German tank production, mounting the powerful 75mm KwK 42 L/70 gun that could penetrate 120mm of armour at 1,094 yards. The main models deployed in Normandy were the Ausf A and Ausf G. Theoretically each I Abteilung of a panzer regiment was equipped with this tank. On the Eastern Front it proved itself superior to the Soviet T-34, though mechanical teething problems initially rendered it unreliable.

Technically the Panther was viewed as one of the best panzers of the Second World War. It proved to be a major menace to Allied armour during 1944–5. Although it did not get off to a terribly good start in 1943 with the Ausf D, by the following year many of its initial problems had been ironed out with the Panther Ausf G. Born of a need to counter the Russian T-34, the winning design had been produced by MAN.

The Panther Ausf D replicated many of the features of the T-34. It had a similar long sloping glacis plate, with inward sloping sides above the tracks. The suspension was provided by interleaved road wheels on transverse torsion bars, which gave a good cross-country ride for the crew. The turret mounted a 75mm L/70 gun that was good for long-distance killing of Allied tanks. The twelve-cylinder Maybach engine developed 642bhp, though this was increased in the later Ausf A and G models to 690bhp, giving a respectable speed of around 28mph.

Defying logic, the initial Ausf D was followed by the Ausf A that incorporated various improvements. Visually the most obvious change was the removal of the crude vertical letterbox-style hull machine-gun mounting in the glacis and replacing it with the conventional ball mount. The turret was also slightly modified: the pistol ports and loading door on the Ausf D were dispensed with and a new type of cupola was fitted.

The last version of the Panther, known as the Ausf G, had further minor modifications, largely to simplify production in the face of shortages of raw materials. Most notably the driver's vision port was replaced with a rotating periscope, thereby increasing the armour integrity of the glacis plate apart from the hull machine-gun ball mount. Also the hull sides were more sloped and the rear stowage boxes were incorporated into the armour of the side skirting plates. The late production models had all steel road wheels instead of the earlier rubber-tyred wheels.

The Panther had a five-man crew, comprising a commander, driver, gunner, loader and radio operator. The driver and radio operator were provided with two periscopes each. Internally the turret had a full cage and could be traversed by hydraulic power or by hand. Despite the technical difficulties endured by the early model Panthers production continued until the very end of the war in May 1945. As a result it was quite a common sight during the fighting in Western Europe until the colse of the war.

The Panther Ausf D seen here was the very first model, seeing action on the Eastern Front and in Italy. On the Western Front the subsequent Ausf A and G were much more common and therefore regularly photographed as wrecks. In Normandy the panzer units were mainly equipped with the Ausf A.

A French woman with a horsedrawn cart passes an abandoned Panther Ausf A somewhere in northern France. She is soothing the animal, which has probably been spooked by drawing near to such a strange roadside behemoth. Coming round the corner to be greeted by this tank would have given any Allied tanker a nasty shock. The Panther served with most of the panzer regiments in Normandy, though few had the full complement of seventeen per company.

A nice iconic shot, if there can be such a thing, of a knocked-out Panther Ausf A in Normandy. The lattice effect on the glacis plate shows the tank has been coated in Zimmerit anti-magnetic paste designed to ward off limpet mines. This was applied in the factory and the finish varied from factor to factory.

*Above:* The very first Panther to be destroyed in the battle for Normandy. On the night of 8/9 June 1944 Panthers of the 12th SS Panzer Division reached Bretteville-l'Orgueilleuse. The lead tank, an Ausf G, was knocked out in the town centre on the rue de Bayeux by the British. It was hit on the rear of the turret with such force that it shattered the 45mm-thick armour. Although the Panthers secured the town, lacking infantry support they withdrew in the morning.

*Opposite above:* Up-ended Panther Ausf A on the outskirts of Norrey-en-Bessin. It would have taken bombers or naval shelling to flip a 45-ton tank like this.

*Opposite below:* Men of the British Durham Light Infantry pose by Panther '204' on 27 June 1944 on the junction of the route between Fontenay-le-Pesnel, Tessel, Rauray and Cheux. It either belonged to the 12th SS or 2nd Panzer Divisions.

*Above:* American P-47 Thunderbolt pilots view one of their victims, a Panther Ausf A on 19 July 1944. Despite their handiwork it looks relatively intact.

*Opposite above:* This Panther with the Panzer Lehr Division was knocked out at le Désert, some 20km north of St Lô on 11 July 1944. The remains of a crewman can be seen on the rear engine deck.

*Opposite below:* More Panzer Lehr Panthers at le Dèsert – comprising two Ausf As abandoned at the roadside. It looks as if they were probably blocking the road and were shunted out of the way. The original caption claimed they were destroyed by the US 9th Infantry Division using anti-tank guns but there are no signs of damage. The driver's vision port is open on the left-hand tank.

*Above:* This photograph was taken on 20 August 1944 just as the Allies were trapping the German army in the Falaise pocket. These US GIs are seated in front of a Panther Ausf A thought to belong to the 116th Panzer Division. It looks to have been abandoned.

*Opposite above:* Yet more Normandy debris. This Panther seems to have been hiding behind the wreckage of a German half-track but succumbed to the American tank destroyer passing through the hedge behind it.

*Opposite below:* Panther Ausf G '322' serving with the independent 106th Panzer Brigade. The Americans found it to the west of Metz in the summer of 1944, its crew having long gone.

This burnt-out Panther was either fighting partially hull-down or managed to get itself well and truly stuck in the mud.

GIs pose with a Panther Ausf G which has suffered a direct hit to the left-hand side.

Late model Ausf G which shed both tracks during the fighting in North-west Europe.

Very late war Panther Ausf G. There is no visible damage to the tank and it may be the case that it simply broke down. Certainly the steel tow bar lying in front of it suggests that this was the case.

*Above:* Two snow-covered Panthers lost during the Ardennes offensive conducted in the winter of 1944–5. Fighting in the confines of the dense forests nullified many of the Panther's advantages. The self-propelled gun in the background to the left is a Sd Kfz 138 armed with a 150mm howitzer.

*Opposite above:* This Ausf G belonged to the 1st SS Panzer Division and was knocked out during the Battle of the Bulge. The tank would have ended up like this thanks to heavy artillery fire or bombers.

*Opposite below:* Another upturned Panther photographed in the winter of 1944–5.

Burnt-out remains of an Ausf G. This was the last model of Panther to be built before the war ended.

The end of the road for this Panther destroyed in late 1944 or early 1945. Two more Panthers are just visible in the background – it is unclear if they are operational.

# CHAPTER TEN

# Tiger I and II

By far the most famous and therefore one of the most often photographed German panzers was the Tiger – or to be more precise the Tiger I. It first saw action in 1942 in the Soviet Union against the Red Army and the following year against the British in Tunisia. Although perhaps best remembered for its role in the Normandy campaign, few actually fought there. The Tiger's deadly 88mm tank gun and its thick armour resulted in it being one of the most feared tanks of the Second World War. American, British and Russian tank crews all developed the habit of describing almost every German tank they encountered as a Tiger.

## Tiger I

Work on Hitler's heavy breakthrough tanks to support the light and medium tanks had commenced in the late 1930s. The requirement to incorporate the 88mm anti-tank gun derived from the anti-aircraft variant resulted in the VK4501 specification. It was the Henschel design that eventually won against the more complex one proposed by Porsche. Although the Tiger was fairly conventional, it featured the use of interleaved road wheels on a tank for the very first time, although they had already been employed on German half-tracks.

As normal, the engine was mounted to the rear, with the transmission led forward via an eight-speed gearbox to the front drive sprockets. The power pack was a V-form twelve-cylinder 650bhp Maybach, though this was increased to 700bhp in the later versions. The engine gave it 24mph which was quite remarkable for a 54-ton tank. The problem with the Tiger was that it was very heavy, over-engineered, costly and time-consuming to build. Although its gun could easily deal with every single type of Allied tank, the Tiger's technological complexity meant it took twice as long to build as the Panther. As a result, only 1,350 were ever built. This was also in part as a result of Allied bombers regularly targeting the Tiger works.

As well as being a breakthrough tank, the Tiger was designed to stand off and kill Allied tanks at great range, but in the confines of the Normandy hedgerows it was unable to play to its strengths in 1944. Following the Battle of Normandy, the survivors were abandoned at the dockside in Rouen.

Many Allied tank crews were soon to develop Tiger anxiety and for good reason. The Tiger could tear a Sherman apart, while the latter could not cope with the Tiger's frontal armour. The American 75mm gun could only penetrate the Tiger at close range and while the British 17-pounder gun was much more effective, it was not available in sufficient numbers. Even those Shermans armed with a 76mm gun had to close to about 300 yards. The Allies only real answer to a Tiger was to overwhelm it or sneak up behind it! However, while the Tiger I was a formidable weapon with 100mm frontal armour and 88mm KwK L/56 gun, only three battalions were deployed in Normandy, with about 126 tanks.

## Tiger II

Likewise the Tiger II proved to be in short supply. The British and Americans dubbed the second version the King or Royal Tiger. This new design featured an even more powerful 88mm anti-tank gun, a sloping glacis plate similar to the Panther and even thicker armour. Development of the Tiger II had been initiated in the autumn of 1942 and drew on combat experience with the Tiger I.

When the Tiger II was delivered to the panzer troops in 1944 it was the most powerful tank in service in the world. This status remained unchanged until almost the very end of the war. However, like the Panther before it, the Tiger II did not have sufficient development time in which to iron out unwelcome teething problems. The net result was that, just like the early Panthers, it was mechanically unreliable. Its weight did not help either, coming in at 14 tons heavier than the Tiger I. While the Tiger II's road wheels overlapped they were not interleaved. Just 485 were ever built.

The Tiger II was brand new in June 1944, but only equipped one company, totalling about a dozen tanks in Normandy. In many ways its high fuel consumption, limited operational range, fragile steering and slow turret traverse nullified its powerful main armament, the 88mm KwK43 L/71, and very thick armour.

Although the Tiger II fought in Normandy and the Ardennes, the close confines of the countryside did not play well to the tank's capabilities. It was designed as a breakthrough tank but its weight inevitably meant that it was consigned to a defensive role. Its size inevitably drew the attention of the Allies. Abandoned and destroyed Tiger IIs were regularly photographed.

A French policeman and local schoolchildren have come to gawp at this Tiger I captured in France in 1944. The American GI standing on the engine grill and the group gathered at the front of the tank would have made sure the Tiger was clear of any booby traps before letting kids play on it. The tank seems to have been haphazardly sprayed to give it a two- or three-tone camouflage. The Tiger I was a well-armed and armoured heavy tank. On the open Russian steppe, it was a very good tank killer, but on the Western Front in the confines of the hedgerows of Normandy and the forested slopes of the Ardennes the Tiger I and II were unable to play to their strengths.

This burnt-out Tiger I was probably shunted off the road after being destroyed. The frayed tow cable to the left suggests attempts may have been made to tow it. The rear of the Tiger was the weakest, with about 26mm of armour.

*Above*: This Tiger I belonged to SS-Obersturmführer Michael Wittman who led the attack on the British 7th Armoured Division at Villers-Bocage on 13 June 1944. He commanded a company of Tiger Is belonging to the 101st Heavy SS-Panzer Battalion. During the street fighting his Tiger was disabled but he and his crew managed to escape. The British then set it alight to stop the Germans from recovering it. Scorch marks are visible on both the hull and turret.

*Opposite above*: Two Tiger Is lost during the battle for Villers-Bocage. After the Germans retook the village it was attacked by the RAF, hence the devastation. The tank in the background belonged to Wittman.

*Opposite below*: This wrecked Tiger I must have an interesting story to tell. Quite why and how it ended up sandwiched between two large log piles is unknown. The stowage bin on the back of the turret has been crushed flat, suggesting a shell impact.

*Above:* The rear of the same Tiger II — both the Bergepanther and the Tiger II were camouflaged with foliage.

*Opposite above:* Tiger II under tow by a Bergepanther armoured recovery vehicle near Vimoutiers captured by the Canadians on 22 August 1944. 1st Company, 503rd Heavy Panzer Battalion had two Bergepanthers on its books. The Tiger II has been torched, most likely by its crew after they could get it no further.

*Opposite below:* Side view of the same vehicles. The fire destroyed part of the ladder attached to the hull. The crew probably acquired this from somewhere to ease clambering up and down from the turret.

*Above*: Another formidable-looking Tiger II lost during the Ardennes offensive. Note the 'ambush' camouflage scheme.

*Opposite above*: It would have taken a considerable blast to split open the belly armour of this Tiger II and turn it over. Strolling past the stranded monster is none other than General Eisenhower, the Allied supreme commander.

*Opposite below*: Numbers of Tiger IIs with the 501st Heavy SS-Panzer Battalion were deployed in support of Hitler's Ardennes offensive in late December 1944. Their weight made them a liability as they were too heavy to use the local bridges, meaning that they were unable to spearhead the attack.

Tiger II '204' was captured by the Americans at La Gleize during the Battle of the Bulge. The Germans left seven Tiger IIs in and around the village. American engineers drove '204' as far as Ruy hoping to get it to the train station at Spa, but it broke down and refused to budge.

The Tiger IIs that fought in the Battle of the Bulge had a very distinctive 'ambush' camouflage scheme. This comprised a sand base colour overpainted with olive green and brown, which was then covered in dots using all three colours.

War's end. One of the last Tiger IIs to be lost, photographed on the streets of Osterode, Germany in April 1945. A puncture hole caused by an American bazooka can be seen on the side of the turret. Note the large 88mm round propped against the turret. It is painted in the Ardennes 'ambush' scheme.

British soldiers pose on the imposing bulk of a Tiger II – its sheer size was its undoing. It also made it a source of fascination for the victorious Allies.

# Other related titles in the Images of War series by Anthony Tucker-Jones